THE VISUAL DICTIONARY

Written by Simon Beecroft

Consultant Jeremy Beckett

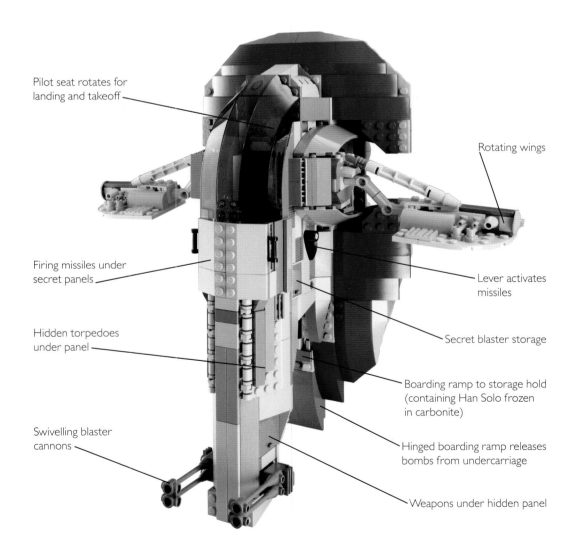

Pilot seat rotates for
landing and takeoff

Rotating wings

Firing missiles under
secret panels

Lever activates
missiles

Hidden torpedoes
under panel

Secret blaster storage

Boarding ramp to storage hold
(containing Han Solo frozen
in carbonite)

Swivelling blaster
cannons

Hinged boarding ramp releases
bombs from undercarriage

Weapons under hidden panel

SLAVE I (2006)

Contents

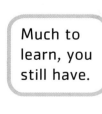

Much to learn, you still have.

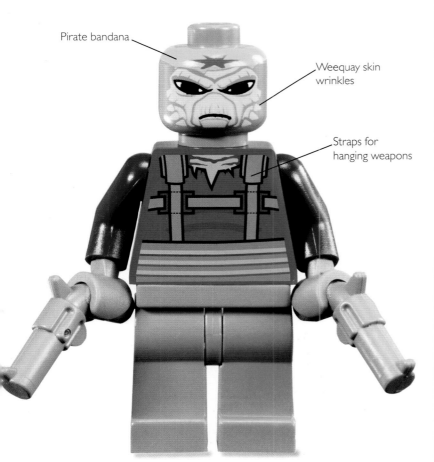

Large, black eyes of Sullustan species

Dewlaps (facial jowls)

Life-support unit

TEN NUMB

Pirate bandana

Weequay skin wrinkles

Straps for hanging weapons

TURK FALSO

Introduction

If *Star Wars* is an extraordinarily rich and detailed fantasy world, LEGO® *Star Wars*™ is that same fantasy world made entirely of coloured bricks. In LEGO *Star Wars*, all the characters, vehicles, settings and weapons of the movies are instantly recognisable, yet subtly different. The wealth of movie-accurate details surprise and delight even the most dedicated *Star Wars* fans: from the targeting sensors on the front of Emperor Palpatine's shuttle to the inclusion of Sullustan B-wing pilot Ten Numb. The LEGO Group's designers are endlessly creative with the lexicon of LEGO elements – a minifigure cup standing in for headlamps on an airspeeder or a green frog from a fairy-tale set becoming a gorg in Jabba's snack bowl. (The only thing more enjoyable is encountering new elements made especially for a LEGO *Star Wars* set: for instance, the printed flap on the cockpit of the Mini AT-ST, which is incredibly simple yet depicts an armour plate, two viewports, and a forward sensor.) But the differences between the movie originals and the LEGO versions are as much fun to spot: a change of colour scheme, a new feature, an interior designed for two minifigures rather than a legion of battle droids. Yes, LEGO *Star Wars* exists in both the *Star Wars* world and the LEGO world, and this is what makes it so fascinating to children and collectors alike.

TIMELINE
The LEGO Group released its first *Star Wars* sets in 1999 to coincide with the release of *Star Wars*: Episode I *The Phantom Menace*. Models were then issued for each new movie in the Prequel Trilogy (Episodes I to III), as well as sets based on the Classic Trilogy and the *Star Wars: The Clone Wars* animated TV show, along with a handful of vehicles from the Expanded Universe (video games, comics, novels, etc.).

DATA BOXES
Throughout the book, each LEGO *Star Wars* set is identified with a data box (see example below), which provides the official name of the set, the year it was first released, the LEGO identification number of the set, the number of LEGO pieces, or elements, in each set (excluding minifigures) and the movies in which the model appears: the abbreviations "EP I" to "EP VI" are used for each of the six movies (EP I, for instance, being *Star Wars*: Episode I *The Phantom Menace*); "CW" is the 2008 animated *Star Wars: The Clone Wars* movie (and ongoing TV show); and "EU" refers to the Expanded Universe.

Set name	Tusken Raider Encounter	
Year 2002	Number	7113
Pieces 90	Film	EP II

1999

Episode I

7101 Lightsaber Duel ▶

◀ 7111 Droid Fighter

7121 Naboo Swamp ▶

◀ 7131 Anakin's Podracer

7141 Naboo Fighter ▶

◀ 7151 Sith Infiltrator

7161 Gungan Sub ▶

◀ 7171 Mos Espa Podrace

2000

◀ 3343 *Star Wars* #4

7115 Gungan Patrol ▶

◀ 7124 Flash Speeder

7155 Trade Federation AAT ▶

◀ 7159 *Star Wars* Bucket

7184 Trade Federation MTT ▶

◀ 8000 Technic Pit Droid

8001 Technic Battle Droid ▶

◀ 8002 Technic Destroyer Droid

LEGO® MINDSTORMS®

9748 Droid Developer Kit ▶

9754 Dark Side Developer Kit ▶

Episode IV

7150 TIE Fighter & Y-Wing ▶

◀ 7110 Landspeeder
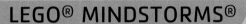

7140 X-Wing Fighter ▶

◀ 7190 *Millennium Falcon*

7191 Ultimate Collector Series X-Wing Fighter ▶

◀ 3340 *Star Wars* #1

7144 *Slave I* ▶

Episode V

7130 Snowspeeder ▶

◀ 3341 *Star Wars* #2

3342 *Star Wars* #3 ▶

◀ 7104 Desert Skiff

Episode VI

7128 Speeder Bikes ▶

◀ 7180 B-Wing at Rebel Control Center

7134 A-Wing Fighter ▶

◀ 7181 Ultimate Collector Series TIE Interceptor

◀ 7126 Battle Droid Carrier

7186 Watto's Junkyard ▶

◀ 10018 Darth Maul

8007 Technic C-3PO ▶

◀ 7106 Droid Escape

7146 TIE Fighter ▶

◀ 10019 Rebel Blockade Runner

8008 Technic Stormtrooper ▶

7166 Imperial Shuttle ▶

◀ 7127 Imperial AT-ST

7203 Jedi Defense I ▶

◀ 7204 Jedi Defense II

10026 Ultimate Collector Series ▶
Naboo Starfighter

Episode II

7103 Jedi Duel ▶

◀ 7113 Tusken Raider Encounter

7133 Bounty Hunter Pursuit ▶

◀ 7143 Jedi Starfighter

7153 Jango Fett's *Slave I* ▶

◀ 7163 Republic Gunship

4487 Mini Jedi Starfighter & *Slave I* ▶

8009 Technic R2-D2 ▶

◀ 8011 Technic Jango

8012 Technic Super Battle Droid ▶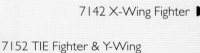

7142 X-Wing Fighter ▶

◀ 7152 TIE Fighter & Y-Wing

◀ 3219 Mini TIE Fighter

8010 Technic Darth Vader ▶

◀ 10030 Ultimate Collector Series
Imperial Star Destroyer

7194 Ultimate Collector Series Yoda ▶

◀ 4486 Mini AT-ST & Snowspeeder

7119 Twin-Pod Cloud Car ▶

7139 Ewok Attack ▶

7200 Final Duel I ▶

◀ 7201 Final Duel II

2003

2004

Episode I

4485 Mini Sebulba's Podracer & Anakin's Podracer ▶

 ◀ 4493 Mini Sith Infiltrator

 ◀ 4491 Mini MTT

4495 Mini AT-TE ▶

Episode II

4478 Geonosian Fighter ▶

 4481 Hailfire Droid ▶

 ◀ 4501 Mos Eisley Cantina

 ◀ 4482 AT-TE

4490 Mini Republic Gunship ▶

7262 TIE Fighter & Y-Wing ▶

Episode IV

 ◀ 4477 T-16 Skyhopper

 ◀ 10131 TIE Fighter Collection

4484 Mini X-Wing Fighter & TIE Advanced ▶

10134 Y-Wing Attack Starfighter ▶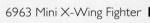

 ◀ 4488 Mini *Millennium Falcon*

 ◀ 4492 Mini Star Destroyer

6963 Mini X-Wing Fighter ▶

Episode V

4479 TIE Bomber ▶

 ◀ 6964 Mini Boba Fett's *Slave I*

4500 Rebel Snowspeeder ▶

4483 AT-AT ▶

4489 Mini AT-AT ▶

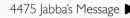 ◀ 10123 Cloud City

 ◀ 4502 X-Wing Fighter

10129 Rebel Snowspeeder ▶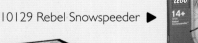

Episode VI

4475 Jabba's Message ▶

 ◀ 4476 Jabba's Prize

4480 Jabba's Palace ▶

◀ 4504 *Millennium Falcon*

 ◀ 4494 Mini Imperial Shuttle

6965 Mini TIE Interceptor ▶

Episode III

6966 Mini Jedi Starfighter ◀

6867 Mini ARC Fighter ▶

 ◀ 6205 V-Wing Fighter

 ◀ 7250 Clone Scout Walker

7251 Darth Vader Transformation ▶

 ◀ 7252 Droid Tri-Fighter

7255 General Grievous Chase ▶

6211 Imperial Star Destroyer ▶

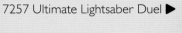 ◀ 7256 Jedi Starfighter & Vulture Droid

7257 Ultimate Lightsaber Duel ▶

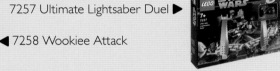 ◀ 7258 Wookiee Attack

◀ 10175 Vader's TIE Advanced

6212 X-Wing Fighter ▶

 ◀ 7259 ARC-170 Starfighter

7260 Wookiee Catamaran ▶

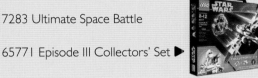 ◀ 7261 Clone Turbo Tank

6209 *Slave I* ▶

 ◀ 7283 Ultimate Space Battle

65771 Episode III Collectors' Set ▶

 ◀ 7263 TIE Fighter

6206 TIE Interceptor ▶

10144 Sandcrawler ▶

 ◀ 6207 A-Wing Fighter

6208 B-Wing Fighter ▶

 ◀ 7264 Imperial Inspection

10143 Death Star II ▶

◀ 6210 Jabba's Sail Barge

 ◀ 6206 TIE Interceptor

10174 Ultimate Collector's ▶
Imperial AT-ST

Episode I

7660 Naboo N-1 Starfighter and Vulture Droid

7662 Trade Federation MTT ▶

◀ 7663 Sith Infiltrator

7665 Republic Cruiser ▶

Episode II

7670 Hailfire Droid & Spider Droid ▶

◀ 7671 AT-AP Walker

10186 General Grievous ▶

◀ 20006 Mini Clone Turbo Tank

◀ 8017 Darth Vader's TIE Fighter

10188 Death Star ▶

◀ 8028 Mini TIE Fighter

Episode III

◀ 7656 General Grievous Starfighter

7661 Jedi Starfighter with Hyperdrive Booster Ring ▶

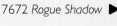

◀ 8029 Mini Rebel Snowspeeder

Episode IV

◀ 7658 Y-Wing Fighter

7668 Rebel Scout Speeder ▶

◀ 7667 Imperial Dropship

7659 Imperial Landing Craft ▶

7672 Rogue Shadow ▶

◀ 10179 Ultimate Collector's Millennium Falcon

Clone Wars

7669 Anakin's Jedi Starfighter ▶

Episode V

◀ 7666 Hoth Rebel Base

10178 Motorized Walking AT-AT ▶

7670 Hailfire Droid & Spider Droid ▶

7673 Magna Guard Starfighter ▶

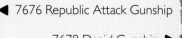

◀ 7674 V-19 Torrent

7675 AT-TE Walker ▶

Episode VI

◀ 7657 AT-ST

◀ 7676 Republic Attack Gunship

7678 Droid Gunship ▶

7679 Republic Fighter Tank ▶

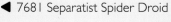

Expanded Universe

7680 The Twilight ▶

7664 TIE Crawler ▶

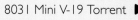

◀ 7681 Separatist Spider Droid

◀ 7654 Droids Battle Pack

8031 Mini V-19 Torrent ▶

7655 Clone Troopers Battle Pack ▶

◀ 20007 Mini Republic Attack Cruiser

 ◄ 7778 Midi-scale *Millennium Falcon*

10198 *Tantive IV* ►

 ◄ 8091 Republic Swamp Speeder

8096 Emperor Palpatine's Shuttle ►

7749 Echo Base ►

 ◄ 8092 Luke's Landspeeder

8099 Midi-scale Imperial Star Destroyer ►

 ◄ 7754 *Home One* Mon Calamari Star Cruiser

8038 The Battle of Endor ►

 ◄ 8083 Rebel Trooper Battle Pack

8084 Snowtrooper Battle Pack ►

◄ 30004 Mini Battle Droid on STAP

30005 Mini Imperial Speeder Bike ►

◄ 8089 Hoth Wampa Cave

8097 *Slave I* ►

◄ 30006 Mini Clone Walker

20009 Mini AT-TE ►

◄ 8129 AT-AT Walker

30051 X-Wing Fighter ►

◄ 20010 Mini Republic Gunship

7748 Corporate Alliance Tank Droid ►

◄ 20018 AT-AT Walker

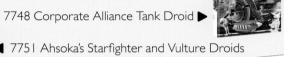 ◄ 7751 Ahsoka's Starfighter and Vulture Droids

7752 Count Dooku's Solar Sailer ►

20016 Imperial Shuttle ►

◄ 7753 Pirate Tank

8014 Clone Walker Battle Pack ►

◄ 8087 TIE Defender

◄ 8015 Assassin Droids Battle Pack

8016 Hyena Droid Bomber ►

 ◄ 8085 Freeco Speeder

8086 Droid Tri-Fighter ►

◄ 8018 AAT

8019 Republic Attack Shuttle ►

◄ 8088 ARC-170 Starfighter

8093 Plo Koon's Jedi Starfighter ►

◄ 8036 Separatist Shuttle

8037 Anakin's Y-Wing Starfighter ►

◄ 8095 General Grievous Starfighter

◄ 8033 Mini General Grievous Starfighter

8039 *Venator*-Class Republic
Attack Cruiser ►

8098 Clone Turbo Tank ►

◄ 8128 Cad Bane's Speeder

 ◄ 10195 Republic Dropship
with AT-OT

30050 Republic Attack Shuttle ►

Anakin Skywalker

Anakin's journey from a slave boy to perhaps the most capable and ambitious Jedi ever is filled with action and danger. Anakin has always been an incredible pilot and has flown everything from 'borrowed' speeders to custom-designed Jedi starfighters during the Clone Wars. But Anakin's daring has its price: The loss of his hand in battle with Count Dooku starts a process of dehumanisation that will end in the full body armour of Darth Vader.

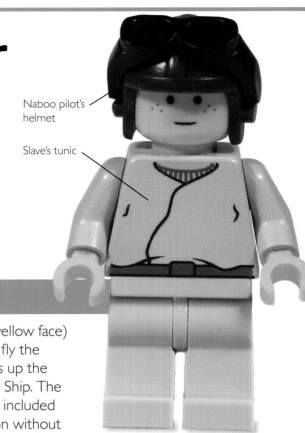

Naboo pilot's helmet

Slave's tunic

YOUNG ANAKIN (IN PILOT HELMET)

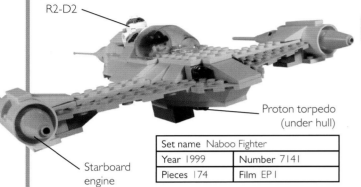

R2-D2

Proton torpedo (under hull)

Starboard engine

◄ Naboo Fighter

Young Anakin Skywalker (with a yellow face) and his trusty astromech, R2-D2, fly the Naboo N-1 starfighter that blows up the Trade Federation's Droid Control Ship. The two blaster-wielding battle droids included with this set are unable to function without the signals from that Control Ship!

Set name	Naboo Fighter	
Year 1999		Number 7141
Pieces 174		Film EP I

▼ Naboo N-1 Starfighter

Set name	Naboo N-1 Starfighter and Vulture Droid	
Year 2007		Number 7660
Pieces 280		Film EP I

Heat-sink finial

Anakin's hair can be swapped with a flying helmet

Hidden missile launcher

Young Anakin Skywalker, in Tatooine robes, now has a natural face colour and short legs (which cannot move). He fits in the cockpit of the starfighter, entering via a boarding ladder. An alternative pilot, a Naboo pilot minifigure, also comes with the set. R2-D2 sits in the droid socket at the back, with a drop-release mechanism that enables him to exit in a hurry! The ship can blast its missile (situated on the underside) at the vulture droid starfighter, also included in the set.

YOUNG ANAKIN

▼ Coruscant Airspeeder

Padawan braid

Teenage Anakin is now a headstrong Padawan, training under Jedi Master Obi-Wan Kenobi. Anakin wears a Padawan braid (printed on his minifigure's shirt.) He and Obi-Wan sit in this airspeeder with its exposed turbojets. The Jedi store their lightsabres in a secret compartment. Can the Jedi catch up with assassin Zam Wessell's speeder, as they weave through the skyscrapers of the city planet, Coruscant?

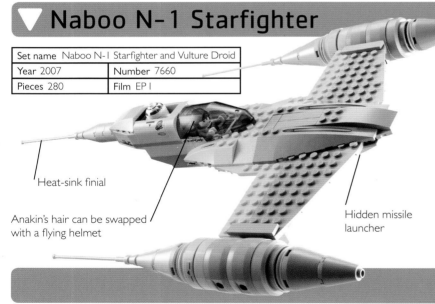

ANAKIN (PADAWAN)

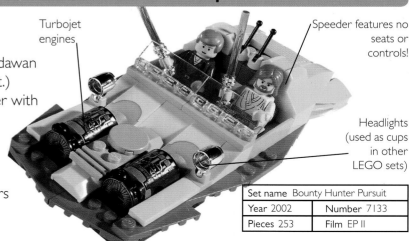

Turbojet engines

Speeder features no seats or controls!

Headlights (used as cups in other LEGO sets)

Set name	Bounty Hunter Pursuit	
Year 2002		Number 7133
Pieces 253		Film EP II

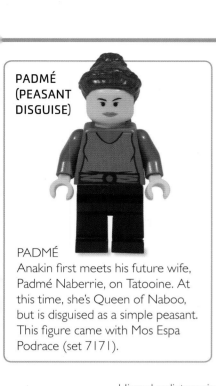

PADMÉ (PEASANT DISGUISE)

PADMÉ
Anakin first meets his future wife, Padmé Naberrie, on Tatooine. At this time, she's Queen of Naboo, but is disguised as a simple peasant. This figure came with Mos Espa Podrace (set 7171).

▼ Swoop Bike

Padawan Anakin borrows Owen Lars's swoop bike to rescue his mother from Tusken Raiders (two are included with the set). The bike has a second seat behind Anakin. Watch out for that moisture vaporator, Anakin! (The vaporator comes with the set and opens to reveal secret controls.)

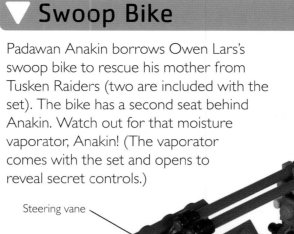

Jedi cloak

Moisture collection bar

Steering vane

Hinged platform

VAPORATOR

Set name	Tusken Raider Encounter	
Year 2002	Number 7113	
Pieces 90	Film EP II	

Hinged radiator wing

Large viewports

Double arc emblem of the Republic fleet

Hinged landing leg

Ion cannon

◀ Jedi Interceptor

Anakin is now a Jedi Knight, with a scarred face, pilot headset, cyborg hand and black robe. He pilots a custom yellow starfighter (actually, an Eta-2 *Actis* Interceptor), with R2-D2 (head only) seated in the astromech socket. Together they fight a fearsome vulture droid (included with the set) — the wings move into attack mode and two blue-tipped missiles can be fired.

Set name	Jedi Starfighter and Vulture Droid	
Year 2005	Number 7256	
Pieces 202	Film EP III	

Force-attuned pilot headset

JEDI ANAKIN
Jedi Knight Anakin, with a black Jedi robe and cyborg hand, appears with the Jedi Starfighter (set 7256) and Ultimate Space Battle (set 7283).

BRICK FACTS

- The Ultimate Lightsaber Duel (set 7257) featured a Jedi Knight Anakin minifigure with a light-up lightsabre to battle Obi-Wan Kenobi (who also has a light-up lightsabre).

- Naboo Fighter (set 7141) came with a small utility vehicle.

UTILITY VEHICLE

Black glove conceals cyborg hand

ANAKIN (JEDI)

13

Obi-Wan Kenobi

For a Jedi who's not crazy about flying, Obi-Wan Kenobi pilots a starfighter a lot of the time — though he can't help losing them, too! Kenobi trains headstrong Anakin Skywalker and goes on missions to far-flung planets including Utapau and Mustafar. Under the Empire, an exiled Obi-Wan meets Luke Skywalker and fights a final duel against his former Padawan, now named Darth Vader.

Padawan braid

OBI-WAN KENOBI (PADAWAN)

▼ Jedi Starfighter

A yellow-faced Kenobi, Jedi Master to Anakin Skywalker, wears a headset when piloting his Delta-7 *Aethersprite* light interceptor. Kenobi's trusty astromech, R4-P17 (styled slightly differently from the movie) provides support. Together, they duel with Jango Fett's *Slave 1*, blasting by the asteroids above Geonosis!

Storage area for lightsabre

OBI-WAN KENOBI (JEDI KNIGHT)

R4-P17 astromech droid (dome only)

Set name	Jedi Starfighter	
Year 2002	Number 7143	
Pieces 138	Film EP II	

Laser cannon

▲ Padawan

In *Star Wars:* Episode I *The Phantom Menace*, Obi-Wan is the Padawan of Jedi Master Qui-Gon Jinn. With a Padawan braid and yellow face, his minifigure battles droidekas two at a time. He wears his Jedi hood when he travels in a Gungan sub and (with a flesh-coloured face) when he flies in the Republic Cruiser.

BRICK FACTS

- Obi-Wan's Padawan minifigure was also issued with a Jedi hood. Obi-Wan "Ben" Kenobi also wore a hood in the Death Star (set 10188). In the Ultimate Lightsaber Duel (set 7257), Kenobi had a light-up lightsabre.

▼ Jedi Interceptor (Red)

During the Battle above Coruscant, Kenobi (with a flesh-coloured face) pilots a red Eta-2 *Actis* Interceptor. This ship is available only in this set, which also includes Anakin's yellow Interceptor, two vulture droids, a tri-fighter, and — watch out, Obi-Wan! — two buzz droids.

Buzz droid

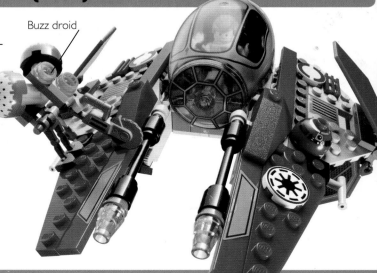

Set name	Ultimate Space Battle	
Year 2005	Number 7283	
Pieces 567	Film EP III	

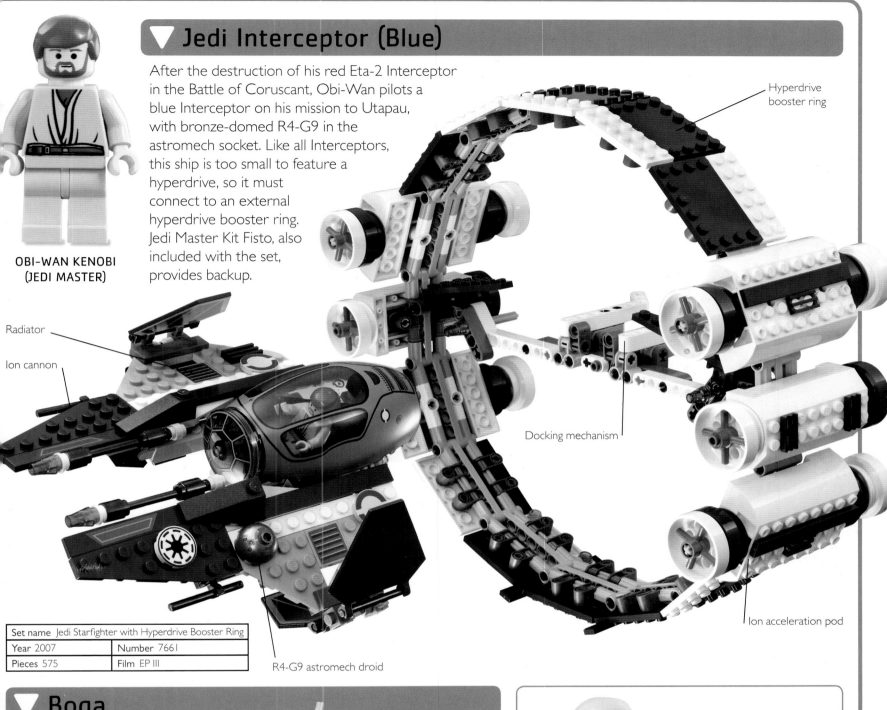

▼ Jedi Interceptor (Blue)

After the destruction of his red Eta-2 Interceptor in the Battle of Coruscant, Obi-Wan pilots a blue Interceptor on his mission to Utapau, with bronze-domed R4-G9 in the astromech socket. Like all Interceptors, this ship is too small to feature a hyperdrive, so it must connect to an external hyperdrive booster ring. Jedi Master Kit Fisto, also included with the set, provides backup.

OBI-WAN KENOBI (JEDI MASTER)

Hyperdrive booster ring

Radiator

Ion cannon

Docking mechanism

Ion acceleration pod

Set name	Jedi Starfighter with Hyperdrive Booster Ring	
Year	2007	Number 7661
Pieces	575	Film EP III

R4-G9 astromech droid

▼ Boga

On Utapau, Obi-Wan rides a fast-moving, reptilian varactyl called Boga to chase General Grievous in his wheel bike. Obi-Wan wears a cloak and carries his blue lightsabre.

Powerful tail

Reins

Clawed feet for climbing

Set name	General Grievous Chase	
Year	2005	Number 7255
Pieces	111	Film EP III

JEDI IN EXILE
In exile on Tatooine, Obi-Wan becomes known as Ben Kenobi. His hair is grey and he wears a cream-coloured Jedi robe. He appears in Luke's landspeeder and at the Mos Eisley cantina, as well as in the *Millennium Falcon* and Death Star (both Ultimate Collector sets).

OBI-WAN "BEN" KENOBI

Jedi Knights

For millennia, the Jedi were the guardians of peace and justice in the galaxy. During the Clone Wars, they become military leaders, fighting alongside clone troopers – in vain. The Sith emerge victorious and the Jedi ranks are decimated. The few remaining Jedi go into hiding until the time comes to restore balance to the Force.

▼ Republic Cruiser

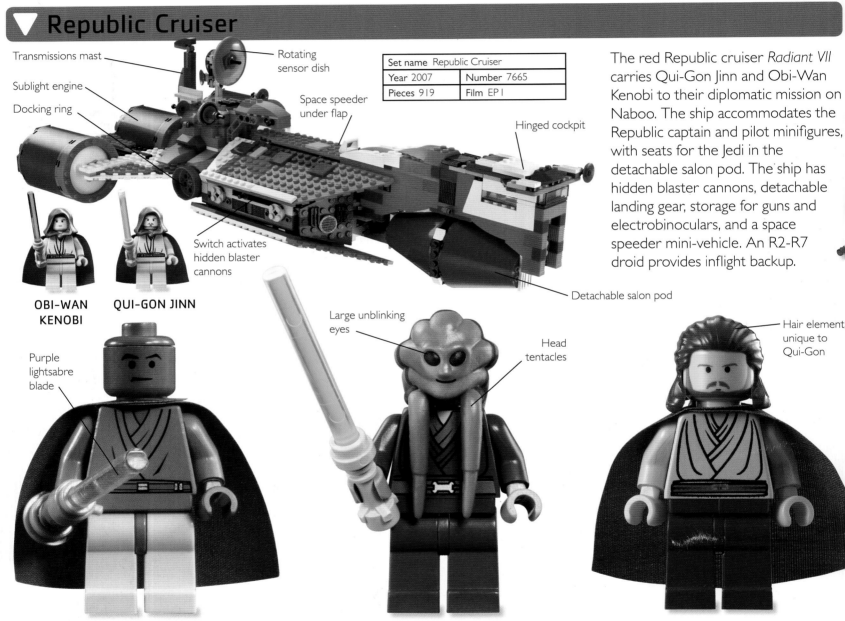

Transmissions mast

Rotating sensor dish

Sublight engine

Docking ring

Space speeder under flap

Hinged cockpit

Set name	Republic Cruiser	
Year 2007		Number 7665
Pieces 919		Film EP1

Switch activates hidden blaster cannons

Detachable salon pod

OBI-WAN KENOBI

QUI-GON JINN

The red Republic cruiser *Radiant VII* carries Qui-Gon Jinn and Obi-Wan Kenobi to their diplomatic mission on Naboo. The ship accommodates the Republic captain and pilot minifigures, with seats for the Jedi in the detachable salon pod. The ship has hidden blaster cannons, detachable landing gear, storage for guns and electrobinoculars, and a space speeder mini-vehicle. An R2-R7 droid provides inflight backup.

Purple lightsabre blade

Large unblinking eyes

Head tentacles

Hair element unique to Qui-Gon

MACE WINDU

A Jedi Master and member of the Jedi Council, Mace Windu is an awesome lightsabre fighter. When he rides in a Clone Turbo Tank, his minifigure wields a rare purple lightsabre, with a light-up blade. However, in the version of this set reissued in 2007, Mace uses a normal lightsabre.

KIT FISTO

Jedi Knight Kit Fisto is a Nautolan, an amphibious species whose head tentacles can sense others' feelings – an ability that can prove useful in combat. During the Clone Wars, Fisto became a member of the Jedi Temple. The head tentacles on his minifigure are made from rubber and he carries a green lightsabre.

QUI-GON JINN

Jedi Qui-Gon Jinn was Padawan to Count Dooku and Master to Obi-Wan. His minifigure fights battle droids on STAPs in the Gungan swamp, combats Darth Maul on Tatooine, rides with Jar Jar and Obi-Wan in a Gungan sub, battles a red security battle droid and flies with Obi-Wan in the Republic cruiser, *Radiant VII*.

Duel on Mustafar

Teetering on service platforms above the red-hot lava of Mustafar, Obi-Wan (wearing a hood, unlike in the movie) fights his former Padawan, Anakin Skywalker, now recruited to the Sith and renamed Darth Vader. They are moved on long rods and their lightsabres glow (though they cannot be removed from the minifigures' hands). Meanwhile the pillars could come crashing down at any time!

Set name	Ultimate Lightsaber Duel	
Year 2005	Number 7257	
Pieces 282	Film EP III	

Orange 'neon' brick

Pillars collapse when pushed

Lava load spills from container

Pole for moving minifigures

Bubbling red-hot lava fountains

Yoda's Hut

Yoda survives the Great Jedi Purge at the end of the Clone Wars to live in exile on Dagobah. He lands on the planet in an escape pod, which he makes into a hut. Yoda's lifestyle on the swamp planet is frugal: His dwelling is furnished with a simple bed, table, cooking pot and barrels.

Native Dagobah foliage

EXTERIOR

Yoda's bed

Yoda carries a gnarled gimer stick, but remains a powerful Jedi Master. You want proof? Just lift his bed to find his secret lightsabre!

Set name	X-Wing Fighter	
Year 2004	Number 4502	
Pieces 563	Film EP V & VI	

Stove

INTERIOR

Large blue eyes of Mirialan species

Grey tunic

LUMINARA UNDULI

Jedi Master Luminara Unduli is a female Mirialan, an exotic humanoid species whose facial tattoos indicate physical accomplishments. Master Unduli fights in the Clone Wars, notably on Kashyyyk, where her minifigure, equipped with a green light-up lightsabre, rides with Yoda on the Wookiee catamaran.

YODA

Grand Master Yoda helps train Dooku before the Count leaves the Jedi Order and joins the Sith. In exile on Dagobah, Yoda teaches Luke Skywalker. His minifigure defends itself against a speeder bike-riding Dooku on Geonosis, and accompanies fellow Jedi Luminara Unduli and Chewbacca on a Wookiee catamaran.

JEDI BOB

The end of the Clone Wars sees most Jedi killed and the Jedi Temple ransacked, with many records lost. All we know about this Jedi (whose name may have been Bob) is that he once flew on a Republic gunship (set 7163).

Sith Apprentices

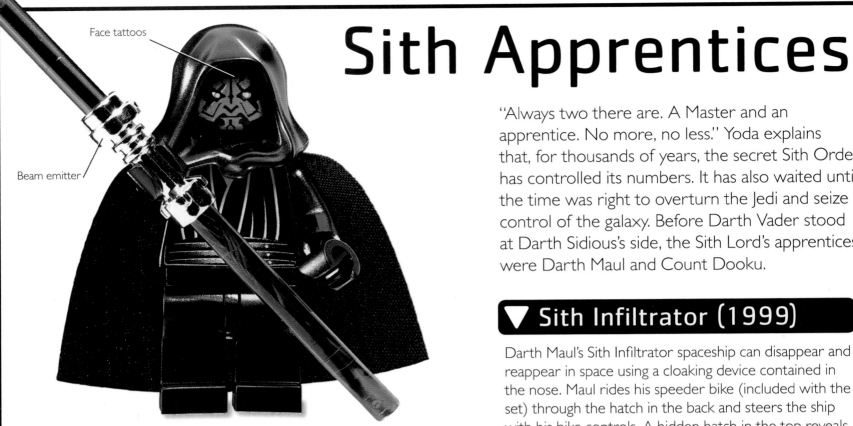

Face tattoos

Beam emitter

DARTH MAUL

"Always two there are. A Master and an apprentice. No more, no less." Yoda explains that, for thousands of years, the secret Sith Order has controlled its numbers. It has also waited until the time was right to overturn the Jedi and seize control of the galaxy. Before Darth Vader stood at Darth Sidious's side, the Sith Lord's apprentices were Darth Maul and Count Dooku.

Darth Maul's minifigure wields a double-bladed lightsabre in Sith Infiltrator (set 7151) and *Star Wars #1* (set 3340.) In Lightsaber Duel (set 7101) and Sith Infiltrator (set 7663), his lightsabre is single-bladed.

▼ Sith Infiltrator (1999)

Darth Maul's Sith Infiltrator spaceship can disappear and reappear in space using a cloaking device contained in the nose. Maul rides his speeder bike (included with the set) through the hatch in the back and steers the ship with his bike controls. A hidden hatch in the top reveals storage for Maul's lightsabre, probe droids and electrobinoculars.

SITH EQUIPMENT
On Tatooine, Darth Maul uses electrobinoculars and 'dark eye' probe droids to search for the Jedi.

Transmission antenna

ELECTROBINOCULARS **PROBE DROID**

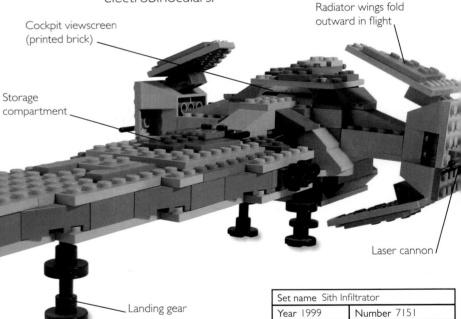

Cockpit viewscreen (printed brick)

Radiator wings fold outward in flight

Storage compartment

Laser cannon

Landing gear

Set name	Sith Infiltrator	
Year 1999	Number 7151	
Pieces 243	Film EP I	

Handgrips

Moisture vaporator

Set name	Lightsaber Duel	
Year 1999	Number 7101	
Pieces 50	Film EP I	

◄ Sith Speeder Bike

Sith apprentice Darth Maul rides an open-cockpit speeder. Powered by a powerful repulsor engine, this super-fast vehicle is highly manoeuvrable, turning at high speed around obstacles such as the moisture vaporator that comes with the set. Darth Maul carries the single lightsabre that he uses to fight Qui-Gon Jinn on Tatooine. The bike and moisture vaporator can be recombined to create a repulsorlift laser blaster platform.

Cockpit roof

Folding radiator wing

Hatch for speeder bike

◀ Sith Infiltrator (2007)

Darth Maul returns in a sleeker version of his Sith Infiltrator, with flick-firing missiles and equipment storage in the nose (for probe droids, electrobinoculars and a lightsabre hilt). Maul's speeder bike drives into the rear of the ship so Maul can operate the flight controls. Two of the ship's weapons can be removed to provide Maul with a double-bladed Sith lightsabre.

Secret storage in engine nose (piece must be removed for access)

Bike uses bricks with knobs on vertical sides

Ship weapons can double as lightsabre blades

SPEEDER BIKE

Set name	Sith Infiltrator	
Year 2007	Number	7663
Pieces 310	Film	EP I

BRICK FACTS

- The Sith minifigure pack, *Star Wars* #1 (set 3340), issued in 2000, featured Darth Maul, Darth Vader (with Anakin's burned face beneath his helmet) and Emperor Palpatine (with a yellow face).

▼ Dooku's Speeder Bike

Count Dooku's open-cockpit repulsorlift speeder bike allows a quick getaway at the Battle of Geonosis – with the Sith Lord carrying the secret plans for the Death Star. In an abandoned factory serving as a hangar for Dooku's Solar Sailer spaceship, Dooku duels with Yoda.

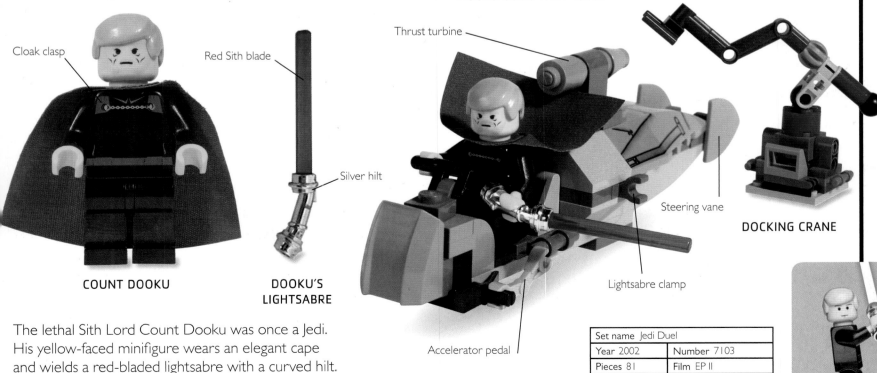

Thrust turbine

Cloak clasp

Red Sith blade

Silver hilt

Steering vane

DOCKING CRANE

COUNT DOOKU

DOOKU'S LIGHTSABRE

Lightsabre clamp

The lethal Sith Lord Count Dooku was once a Jedi. His yellow-faced minifigure wears an elegant cape and wields a red-bladed lightsabre with a curved hilt.

Accelerator pedal

Set name	Jedi Duel	
Year 2002	Number	7103
Pieces 81	Film	EP II

Podracing

Ladies and gentlemen, Dugs and Hutts, please join us at the Boonta Eve Classic, the most keenly fought and downright dangerous Podrace on Tatooine. Experienced racers Sebulba, Gasgano and Aldar Beedo will power up their oversized Podracers, while human newcomer, nine-year-old Anakin Skywalker, climbs aboard his self-made machine, watched nervously by his supporters. The tension here is electric!

▼ Starters' Box

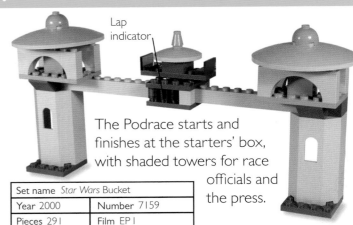

Lap indicator

The Podrace starts and finishes at the starters' box, with shaded towers for race officials and the press.

Set name	Star Wars Bucket	
Year 2000	Number 7159	
Pieces 291	Film EP I	

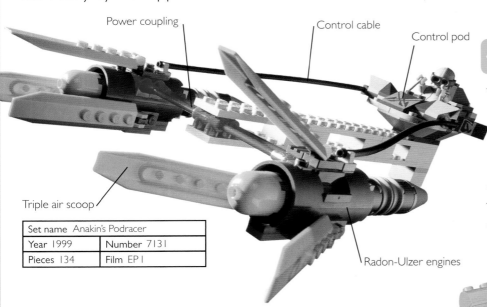

Power coupling

Control cable

Control pod

Triple air scoop

Radon-Ulzer engines

Set name	Anakin's Podracer	
Year 1999	Number 7131	
Pieces 134	Film EP I	

◄ Anakin's Podracer

What's that blur on the Tatooine horizon? It's Anakin, in flying goggles, piloting his super-fast Podracer, with 'glowing' power couplings and hinged front air scoops (for additional control in cornering). If Anakin needs any help fine-tuning or repairing his vehicle, a pit droid is on hand. Padmé hopes that Anakin will at least survive the dangerous enterprise.

ANAKIN SKYWALKER (PODRACER)

Afterburner

► Sebulba's Podracer

The dastardly Dug named Sebulba is determined to win the Boonta Eve Classic — and he doesn't care what dirty tricks he uses to do so. Sebulba's Podracer has four secret flip-up weapons, including a deadly chainsaw, along with six opening flaps on the engine nozzles. His pit droid stands by at its repair station.

SEBULBA

Illegal weapon

Energy binder

BRICK FACTS

- Aldar Beedo appeared in two forms. In the *Star Wars* Bucket (set 7159, from 2000), he was made from battle droid pieces: His head had a breathing mask and pilot's helmet. But in Watto's Junkyard (set 7186, from 2001), he had a custom mould.

ALDAR BEEDO (2000)

PIT DROID
These droid mechanics are fast workers, but are quite accident-prone. They see by using a single photoreceptor, while their head plates protect them from bumps.

PIT DROID

Race decal

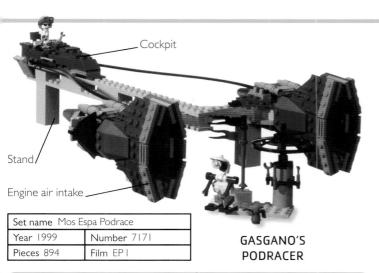

Cockpit

Stand

Engine air intake

Set name	Mos Espa Podrace	
Year 1999	Number 7171	
Pieces 894	Film EP I	

GASGANO'S
PODRACER

▲ Gasgano's Podracer

GASGANO

Gasgano pilots a custom Ord Pedrovia Podracer, with huge engine-mounted air intakes designed to cool down the overheated craft. He uses all his six arms to pilot the machine at extraordinary speeds (four are seen on the minifigure; two are hidden, working the foot controls), taking second place in the Boonta Eve Classic. His Podracer has two flip-up weapons and moving anti-turbulence vanes.

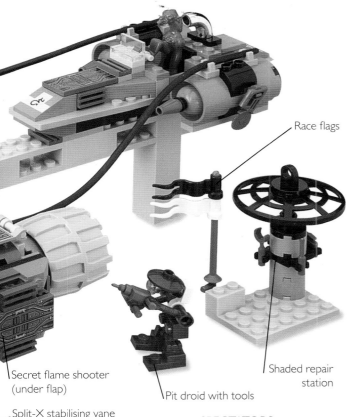

Race flags

Secret flame shooter
(under flap)

Split-X stabilising vane

Pit droid with tools

Shaded repair
station

Set name	Mos Espa Podrace	
Year 1999	Number 7171	
Pieces 894	Film EP I	

SPECTATORS
In addition to pit droids, the Mos Espa Podrace set includes Qui-Gon Jinn, Padmé Amidala, Jar Jar Binks, C-3PO and R2-D2, all watching with bated breath.

▼ Watto's Junkyard

Podracer pilots on Tatooine all know about Watto's junkyard, where they can find a spare part or custom accessory, even if the winged Toydarian strikes a hard bargain. Look, there's Aldar Beedo now, looking for ways to add speed and manoeuvrability to his Mark IV Flat-Twin Turbojet Podracer. Mawhonic's Ord Pedrovia Podracer is here, too, souped up with scrounged parts, though this won't stop Sebulba from ramming the craft until it crashes in the race.

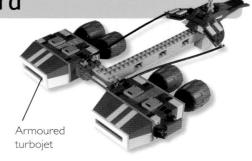

Armoured
turbojet

ALDAR BEEDO'S PODRACER

Set name	Watto's Junkyard	
Year 2001	Number 7186	
Pieces 466	Film EP I	

Secondary
thruster

MAWHONIC'S PODRACER

ALDAR BEEDO   WATTO

Junkyard parts can also
form a stand for
Mawhonic's Podracer

WATTO'S JUNKYARD

▼ Other Podracers

Lined up and ready to race: Simplified versions of Anakin's and Aldar Beedo's Podracers rev up alongside Neva Kee's experimental machine, with its cockpit placed in front of the massive engines (which could be dangerous!), and Clegg Holdfast's Volvec KT9 Wasp Podracer, with a winged protective canopy over its cockpit.

ALDAR
BEEDO'S
PODRACER

ANAKIN'S
PODRACER

NEVA KEE'S
PODRACER

Canopy over
command chair

CLEGG
HOLDFAST'S
PODRACER

Set name	Star Wars Bucket	
Year 2000	Number 7159	
Pieces 291	Film EP I	

Naboo and Gungans

It takes an invasion by the villainous Trade Federation to propel peaceful Naboo to consider war. Its inhabitants — human Naboo and amphibious Gungans — must band together and work with their Jedi protectors to repel the hordes of merciless battle droids.

Energy shield

Feathers indicate status

Battle wagon

Saddle made of fambaa skin

Energy ball

Billed snout

Set name	Gungan Patrol	
Year 2000	Number 7115	
Pieces 77	Film EP I	

▼ Naboo Swamp

Jedi Qui-Gon Jinn and Obi-Wan Kenobi land on Naboo to help its inhabitants. In the Naboo swamp, Qui-Gon Jinn uses his lightsabre to deflect blaster fire from battle droids on STAPs (Single Trooper Aerial Platforms) and shield his Gungan guide, Jar Jar Binks. The STAPs come with 'invisible' stands to make them hover.

JAR JAR BINKS

Dense foliage

Twin blasters

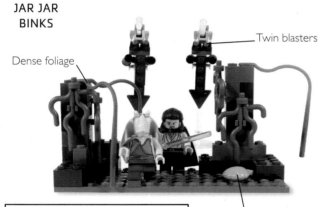

Set name	Naboo Swamp	
Year 1999	Number 7121	
Pieces 81	Film EP I	

Swamp clam

▲ Gungan Patrol

Gungans ride large, flightless kaadu. These amphibious animals are fast and agile. Many kaadu are used as beasts of burden, though larger four-legged falumpasets are also popular. These two kaadu, ridden by Jar Jar Binks and a Gungan soldier, pull wagons carrying energy-ball ammunition into battle against the droid army. The energy balls roll out of the back of the wagon.

▼ Flash Speeder

A Naboo security officer pilots a repulsorlift flash speeder, one of the ground craft used for patrols in peacetime, but employed in the defence of Theed Palace during the invasion of Naboo.

Blaster (secret compartment beneath)

Twin-seat model

Set name	Flash Speeder	
Year 2000	Number 7124	
Pieces 105	Film EP I	

Wing-mounted engines

▶ Gungan Sub

Qui-Gon Jinn, Obi-Wan Kenobi, and Jar Jar Binks travel to Theed from the underwater city of Otoh Gunga in a bongo, or Gungan sub. The set adapts the movie's three-person cockpit model to a version with three cockpits. Lurking underwater are a manta ray, a clam and a starfish (staples of earlier deep-sea or beach LEGO sets). The set's instructions provide ideas (and a comic strip) for several variant models, including a submersible, a spaceship, a lifeboat and a 'monster' sub to scare sea creatures!

Rotating drive fins

Compartment for alternate engines

Compartment for rudder

Forward cockpit bubble

Forward diving plane

Set name	Gungan Sub	
Year 1999	Number 7161	
Pieces 375	Film EP I	

Geonosians

▼ Geonosian Fighter

Thousands of deadly *Nantex*-class starfighters are launched against Republic forces at the Battle of Geonosis. These ships are specially designed to accommodate the anatomy of Geonosian pilots, and include a lifting cockpit roof, hinged steps and a swivelling forward laser cannon.

During the Clone Wars, the hive-dwelling Geonosians are notorious for their huge factories that endlessly churn out battle droids for the Separatist Army. A winged elite class rules over this savage, caste-based society, with wingless drones doing all the work. Geonosian soldiers carry exotic sonic weapons and fly twin-pronged fighter ships.

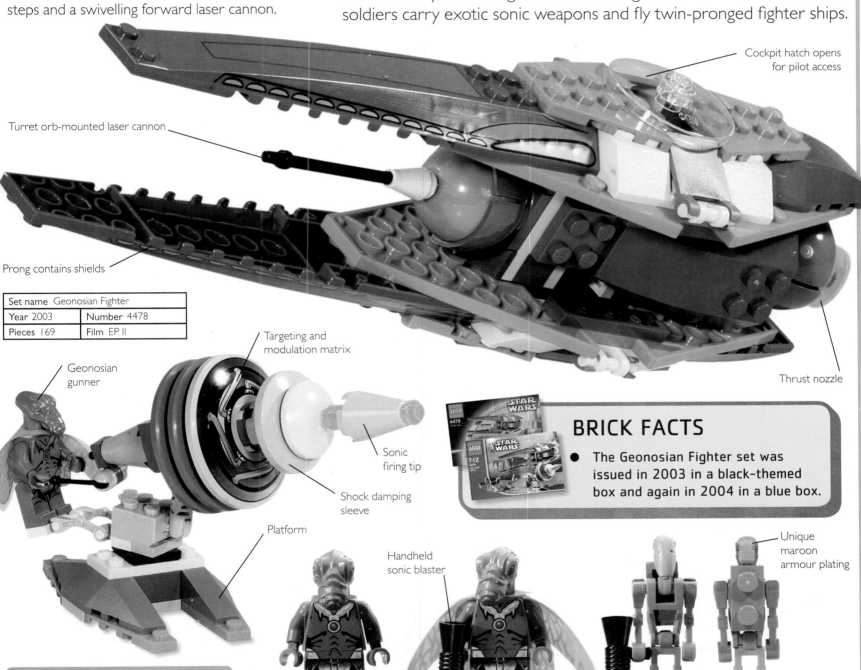

Cockpit hatch opens for pilot access

Turret orb-mounted laser cannon

Prong contains shields

Set name	Geonosian Fighter	
Year 2003	Number 4478	
Pieces 169	Film EP II	

Geonosian gunner

Targeting and modulation matrix

Thrust nozzle

Sonic firing tip

Shock damping sleeve

Platform

BRICK FACTS

- The Geonosian Fighter set was issued in 2003 in a black-themed box and again in 2004 in a blue box.

Handheld sonic blaster

Unique maroon armour plating

▲ Sonic Cannon

Geonosian soldiers deploy both handheld sonic blasters and platform-mounted sonic cannons. These weapons fire balls of high-impact concussive energy.

DRONE

Wingless drones do all the manual labour in Geonosian society.

WARRIOR

Winged Geonosians are an elite caste that includes warriors.

BATTLE DROIDS

The Geonosian Fighter set includes two sandy-red Geonosian-issue droids.

Bounty Hunters

Bounty hunters track down and capture people in order to collect a fee, or bounty. These ruthless, capable hunters prefer to work alone, but occasionally they hire fellow professionals such as assassin Zam Wesell. Two of the most legendary bounty hunters in the galaxy are Jango Fett and his son, Boba Fett.

Targeting rangefinder

Jetpack

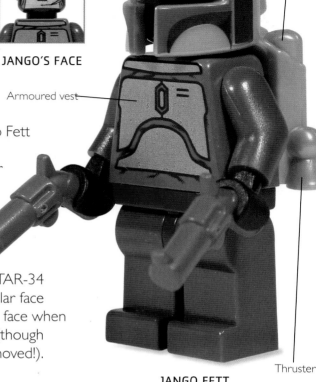

JANGO'S FACE

Armoured vest

▲ Jango Fett's *Slave I*

Repulsorlift wing

Cockpit console

Bounty hunter Jango Fett wears distinctive Mandalorian armour (Mandalorians were the best mercenaries in the galaxy) and carries custom-made WESTAR-34 blasters. Jango's regular face can swivel to a black face when wearing his helmet (though his hair must be removed!).

Thruster

JANGO FETT

Wing support strut

Fold-out blasters

COCKPIT INTERIOR

Twin blaster cannons

YOUNG BOBA FETT
The Republic based its first clone army on the genetic material of Jango Fett, who, as a supreme warrior, was hired for a fee. As part of his deal with the Kaminoan cloners, Jango is allowed one unaltered clone to be his son, Boba. The Boba minifigure has a determined expression and half-size legs, which don't bend.

Set name	Jango Fett's *Slave I*
Year 2002	Number 7153
Pieces 358	Film EP II & V

Jango Fett's *Slave I* is bristling with weapons, many of which are hidden to deliver devastating surprise assaults. The armaments consist of two four-barrel fold-out blaster cannons, twin rotating laser cannons, two concealed heat-seeking rocket launchers and three drop bombs, as well as a removable prisoner cage. A smuggling box can be magnetically attached to the underside of the ship. When the repulsorlift wings swivel, they rotate the cockpit from landing to flight mode.

BRICK FACTS

- Boba Fett also comes with *Star Wars #2* (set 3341), along with Luke Skywalker and Han Solo, as well as Jabba's Prize (set 4476), Jabba's Sail Barge (set 6210) and, with printed legs, Cloud City (set 10123).

BOBA FETT

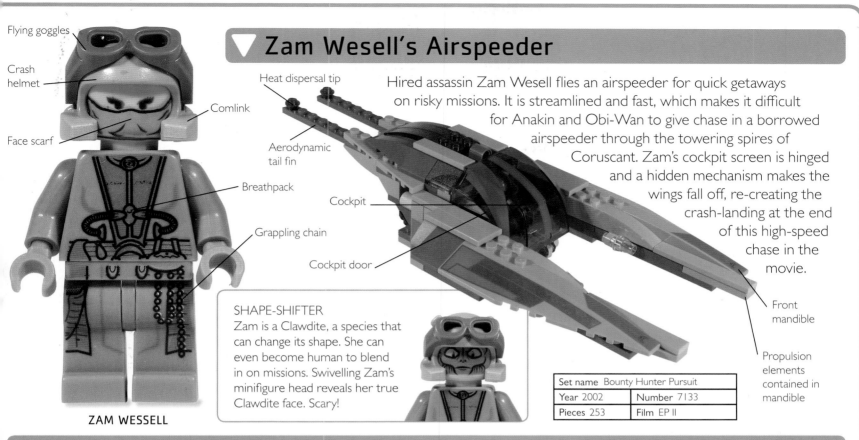

▼ Zam Wesell's Airspeeder

Flying goggles

Crash helmet

Face scarf

Comlink

Heat dispersal tip

Aerodynamic tail fin

Breathpack

Cockpit

Grappling chain

Cockpit door

Hired assassin Zam Wesell flies an airspeeder for quick getaways on risky missions. It is streamlined and fast, which makes it difficult for Anakin and Obi-Wan to give chase in a borrowed airspeeder through the towering spires of Coruscant. Zam's cockpit screen is hinged and a hidden mechanism makes the wings fall off, re-creating the crash-landing at the end of this high-speed chase in the movie.

Front mandible

Propulsion elements contained in mandible

SHAPE-SHIFTER
Zam is a Clawdite, a species that can change its shape. She can even become human to blend in on missions. Swivelling Zam's minifigure head reveals her true Clawdite face. Scary!

ZAM WESSELL

Set name	Bounty Hunter Pursuit	
Year	2002	Number 7133
Pieces	253	Film EP II

▶ Boba Fett's *Slave I*

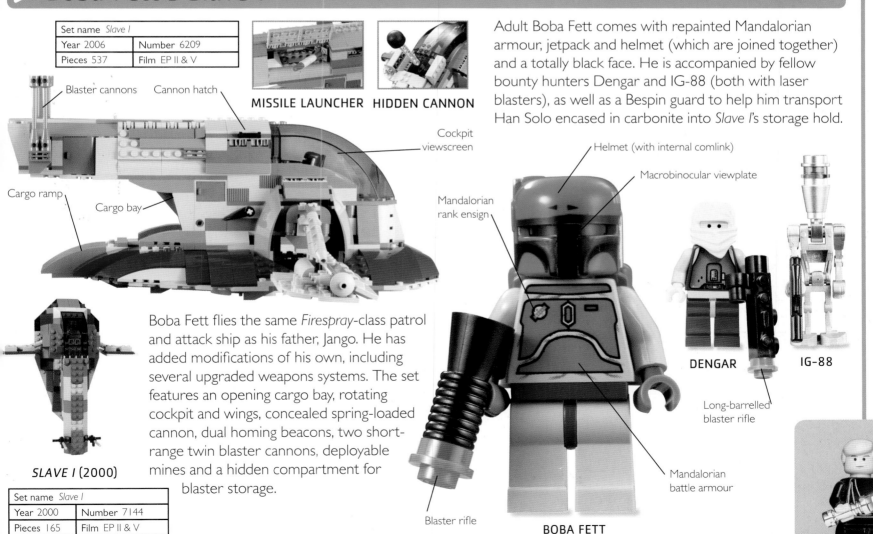

Set name	*Slave I*	
Year	2006	Number 6209
Pieces	537	Film EP II & V

Blaster cannons

Cannon hatch

MISSILE LAUNCHER **HIDDEN CANNON**

Cockpit viewscreen

Cargo ramp

Cargo bay

Adult Boba Fett comes with repainted Mandalorian armour, jetpack and helmet (which are joined together) and a totally black face. He is accompanied by fellow bounty hunters Dengar and IG-88 (both with laser blasters), as well as a Bespin guard to help him transport Han Solo encased in carbonite into *Slave I*'s storage hold.

Helmet (with internal comlink)

Macrobinocular viewplate

Mandalorian rank ensign

DENGAR

IG-88

Long-barrelled blaster rifle

Boba Fett flies the same *Firespray*-class patrol and attack ship as his father, Jango. He has added modifications of his own, including several upgraded weapons systems. The set features an opening cargo bay, rotating cockpit and wings, concealed spring-loaded cannon, dual homing beacons, two short-range twin blaster cannons, deployable mines and a hidden compartment for blaster storage.

Mandalorian battle armour

SLAVE I (2000)

Set name	*Slave I*	
Year	2000	Number 7144
Pieces	165	Film EP II & V

Blaster rifle

BOBA FETT

Separatist Army

Although mass armies are illegal at the start of the Clone Wars, many wealthy commercial bodies use private forces to enforce payments and collect debts. These armies are pooled to form the Separatist army, which begins to wage deadly war across the galaxy.

▼ Armoured Assault Tank

Trade Federation battle tanks, called AATs (Armoured Assault Tanks), are repulsorlift tanks carrying massive forward-facing guns. A pilot droid in the forward seat drives the tank into battle, with a second battle droid acting as gunner in the top hatch. AATs spearhead the invasion of Naboo, rolling into Theed to take the Palace and meeting the Gungan army on the grass plains.

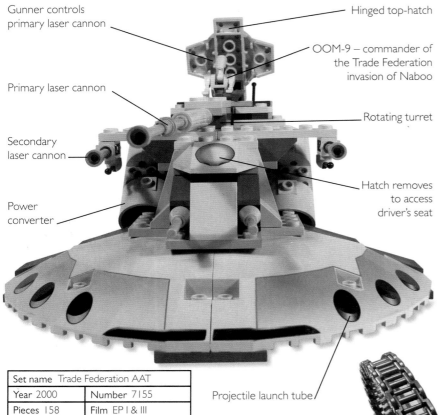

Gunner controls primary laser cannon

Hinged top-hatch

OOM-9 – commander of the Trade Federation invasion of Naboo

Primary laser cannon

Secondary laser cannon

Rotating turret

Power converter

Hatch removes to access driver's seat

Projectile launch tube

Set name	Trade Federation AAT	
Year 2000		Number 7155
Pieces 158		Film EP I & III

▶ Hailfire Droid

Hailfire droids roll into battle on giant hoop wheels while firing deadly heat-seeking missiles from two top-mounted racks.

Set name	Hailfire Droid and Spider Droid	
Year 2008		Number 7670
Pieces 249		Film EP II

Cockpit

Hinged troop hatch

Twin blaster cannons

Set name	Trade Federation MTT	
Year 2000		Number 7184
Pieces 466		Film EP I & III

▲ MTT (2000)

When the Trade Federation invades Naboo, it transports platoons of ground troops in huge MTTs (Multi Troop Transports, or, simply, large transports). This model can hold six battle droids, deployed via a sliding rack system from the hinged front hatch. Side doors open to reveal a storage compartment and a control room with a pilot seat. The back hatch opens to fire the forward blaster cannons.

BRICK FACTS

- The Trade Federation MTT (set 7662, released in 2007) was the first set to include battle droid minifigures with turned hands that could hold a standard blaster. The set also included a redesigned droideka.

- The Hailfire Droid & Spider Droid (set 7670) first appeared in movie-related box packaging in January 2008. It was reissued in Clone Wars packaging in September 2008.

Photoreceptor

Missile launchers

Hoop wheel

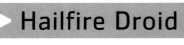

▶ MTT (2007)

The larger, updated MTT carries 20 battle droids. Turning the side gear deploys the droid storage rack, while various exterior panels are hinged to allow access to the interior. A separate troop carrier deploys from a hatch in the back for the rapid transport of battle-ready droids. The set includes 16 regular battle droids, two red security droids, two blue pilot droids and a droideka.

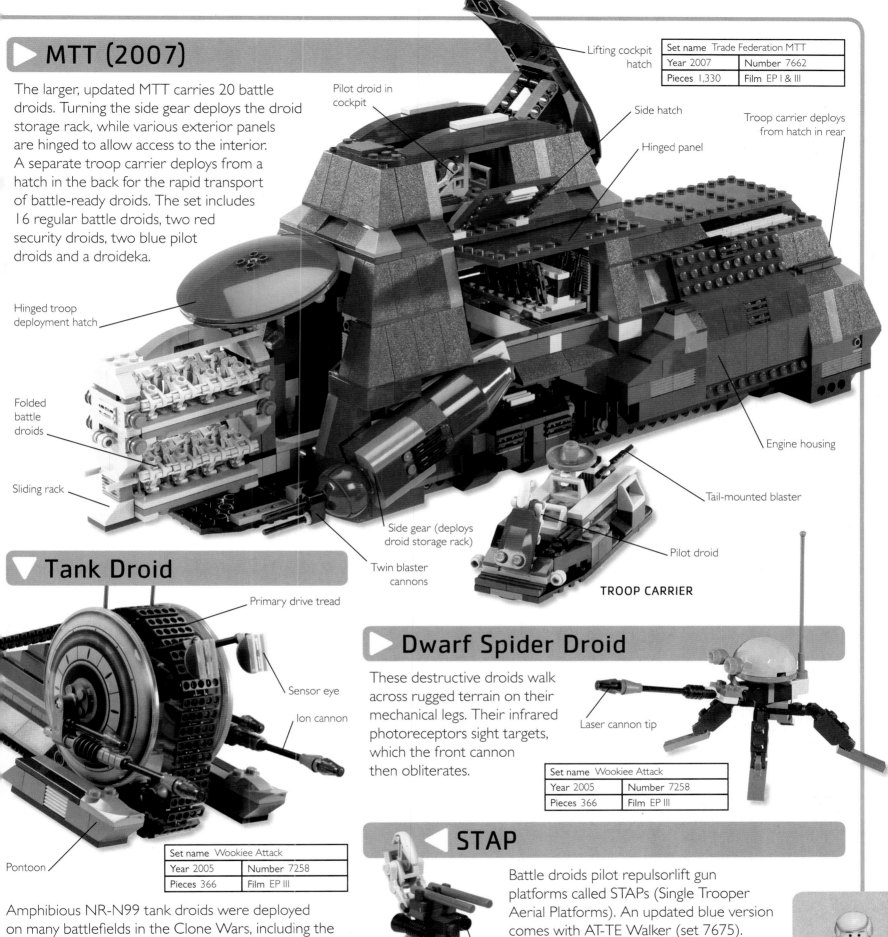

Pilot droid in cockpit

Lifting cockpit hatch

Side hatch

Hinged panel

Troop carrier deploys from hatch in rear

Set name	Trade Federation MTT	
Year 2007		Number 7662
Pieces 1,330		Film EP I & III

Hinged troop deployment hatch

Folded battle droids

Sliding rack

Side gear (deploys droid storage rack)

Twin blaster cannons

Engine housing

Tail-mounted blaster

Pilot droid

TROOP CARRIER

▼ Tank Droid

Primary drive tread

Sensor eye

Ion cannon

Pontoon

Amphibious NR-N99 tank droids were deployed on many battlefields in the Clone Wars, including the Wookiee planet, Kashyyyk. Their treads provide good traction on land or water-logged surfaces. The sensor 'eyes' locate targets and the forward guns fire ion-charged missiles.

Set name	Wookiee Attack	
Year 2005		Number 7258
Pieces 366		Film EP III

▶ Dwarf Spider Droid

These destructive droids walk across rugged terrain on their mechanical legs. Their infrared photoreceptors sight targets, which the front cannon then obliterates.

Laser cannon tip

Set name	Wookiee Attack	
Year 2005		Number 7258
Pieces 366		Film EP III

◀ STAP

Battle droids pilot repulsorlift gun platforms called STAPs (Single Trooper Aerial Platforms). An updated blue version comes with AT-TE Walker (set 7675).

Side thruster

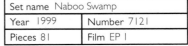

Set name	Naboo Swamp	
Year 1999		Number 7121
Pieces 81		Film EP I

27

Separatist Navy

After their first success at the Battle of Geonosis, Separatist forces plot and scheme even greater exploits. The gigantic space battle above Coruscant, in which General Grievous attempts to kidnap Supreme Chancellor Palpatine, sees the use of a deadly range of specialised droid fighters.

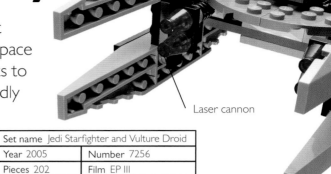

Active sensor 'eyes'

Laser cannon

Set name Jedi Starfighter and Vulture Droid	
Year 2005	Number 7256
Pieces 202	Film EP III

▽ Droid Fighter (1999)

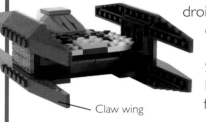

Claw wing

Swarms of pilot-less droid fighters (or Vulture droid fighters) are unleashed against enemies. They are controlled by signals from a central Droid Control Ship computer. The wings become legs when deployed as walking fighters (though, on this set, they do not move in walk mode). This easy-to-build set foregoes some details, like weapons, for simplicity and playability.

Set name Droid Fighter	
Year 1999	Number 7111
Pieces 62	Film EP 1

▲ Vulture Droid (2005)

The droid fighter transforms in a few clicks from flight mode to walk mode. This time, the legs move in walk mode and the fighter features simple laser weapons.

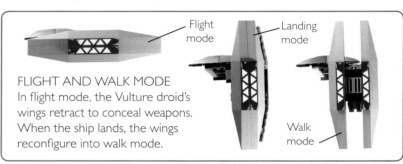

Flight mode

Landing mode

Walk mode

FLIGHT AND WALK MODE
In flight mode, the Vulture droid's wings retract to conceal weapons. When the ship lands, the wings reconfigure into walk mode.

▷ Vulture Droid (2007)

This version of the Vulture droid starfighter battles Anakin Skywalker in his Naboo N-1 starfighter. The droid's missiles are operated by a flick-firing mechanism and the ship converts into flying, attack and walking modes (with a neck strut that enables the head to swivel).

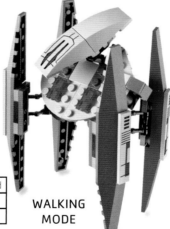

WALKING MODE

Set name Naboo N-1 Starfighter and Vulture Droid	
Year 2007	Number 7660
Pieces 280	Film EP 1

▽ Droid Tri-Fighter

With a nose-mounted laser cannon and three light laser cannons, droid tri-fighters are deadlier than Vulture droids. These agile, fast droids excel at dogfights with Republic starfighters. This modified tri-fighter carries a buzz-droid missile in its central sphere.

Firing mechanism

Set name Droid Tri-Fighter	
Year 2005	Number 7252
Pieces 148	Film EP III

BRICK FACTS

● An Episode III Collectors' Set (65771) also included the droid tri-fighter and a buzz droid, as well as an ARC-170 starfighter, mini Jedi starfighter or mini ARC fighter, plus three clone pilots and an R2 unit, an Episode III LEGO poster and a CD-ROM, 'From the LEGO Vaults'.

BUZZ DROID
Guided buzz-droid missiles burst open in the vicinity of enemy ships to launch buzz droids armed with cutters and graspers, which they then use to attack the nearby craft. Buzz droids are small enough to slip through a target ship's shields and they carry schematics in their droid 'brains' to identify a ship's weak points.

BUZZ DROID

General Grievous

The Supreme Commander of the Droid Armies is a villainous cyborg called General Grievous. Grievous does not consider himself a droid, however – and reacts savagely to anyone who calls him one. His hatred of the Jedi Knights in particular is long-standing and all-consuming. His only pleasure is defeating Jedi in battle and collecting their lightsabres as trophies.

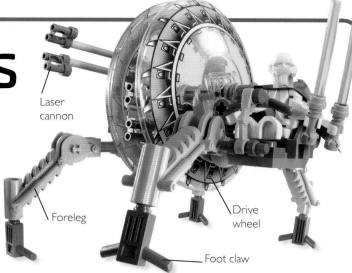

Laser cannon

Foreleg

Drive wheel

Foot claw

WALKING MODE

Two green and two blue lightsabres

Carved skull mask

Arms split into four

GRIEVOUS WITH CAPE

In General Grievous Chase (set 7255) Grievous wears a cape and wields lightsabres. In General Grievous Starfighter (set 7656), he has lightsabres and a blaster but no cape.

GRIEVOUS WITH BLASTER

▲ Wheel Bike

On Utapau, General Grievous rides a wheel bike, designed to achieve intimidating high speeds across hard terrain. If obstacles block its path, no problem: Its two pairs of legs just walk over them! The set comes with Obi-Wan on a giant lizard – and a rare minifigure of Grievous with his cape.

Set name	General Grievous Chase	
Year 2005	Number 7255	
Pieces 111	Film EP III	

WHEEL MODE

▼ Grievous's Starfighter

General Grievous's battle-worn Belbullab-22 fighter is hyperdrive-capable, and features a sliding cockpit, folding tail landing gear, a lightsabre holder, and flip-up laser cannons. (The landing gear and lightsabres can be stored under the craft for flight).

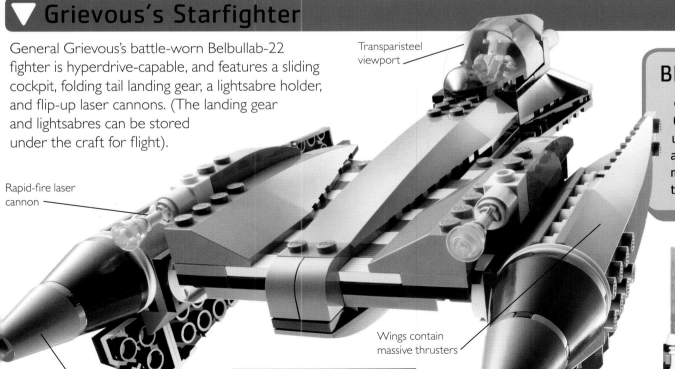

Transparisteel viewport

Rapid-fire laser cannon

Wings contain massive thrusters

Forward scanner

Set name	General Grievous Starfighter	
Year 2007	Number 7656	
Pieces 232	Film EP III	

BRICK FACTS

● The General Grievous minifigure utilises the same legs as the battle droid minifigure, except they are white.

LIGHTSABRE RACK

29

Battle Droids

Battle droids are the foot soldiers of the Separatist Army. The advantage of these mindless mechanised soldiers is that they can be manufactured easily and cheaply in huge factories on planets such as Geonosis. Basic battle droids have no independent thought processors, although upgraded versions, such as commanders and super battle droids, are able to make limited independent tactical decisions.

Arm with turned hand to hold blaster

Optical sensor

Magnetic-grip foot

WITHOUT BACKPACK

WITH BACKPACK

◀ Infantry Battle Droid

Infantry battle droids make up the majority of the Separatist land troops. Early versions have two identical hands. From 2007 onwards, battle droid minifigures have a turned hand in order to hold a blaster properly.

▼ Droid Commander

Commanders operate with a degree of autonomy compared to the standard infantry. They come in two versions, one with a partially yellow chest and the other with a completely yellow chest.

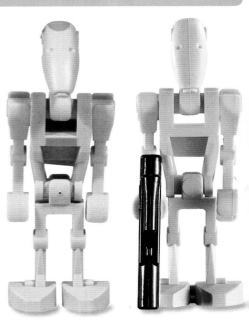

Targeting scope

◀ Security Droid

This model of battle droid specialises in basic security tasks, including patrols and guarding prisoners. They are denoted by the dark-red colouring on their chests.

▶ Pilot Droid

Blue chest colouration identifies pilot droids. These specialist droids control various vehicles, including MTTs and battle droid carriers.

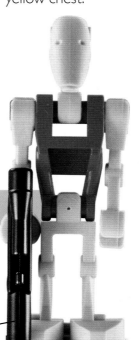

SE-14 blaster pistol

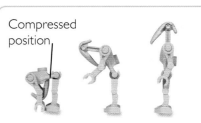

Compressed position

COLLAPSIBLE SOLDIERS
Battle droid minifigures fold up for efficient storage in deployment racks in MTTs and other carriers.

Super Battle Droid

Super battle droids are larger, stronger versions of regular battle droids. They are equipped with tougher armour. A metal-blue version came with the Republic Gunship (set 7163, from 2002). A dark-grey version came with the Droids Battle Pack (set 7654, from 2007) and the Hailfire Droid & Spider Droid (set 7670, from 2008).

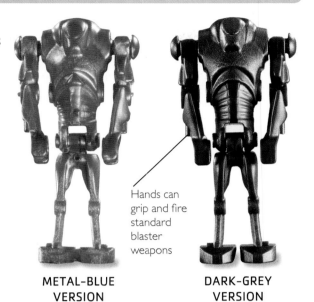

Hands can grip and fire standard blaster weapons

METAL-BLUE VERSION

DARK-GREY VERSION

Blasters

ION PISTOL

SE-14 BLASTER PISTOL

E-5 BLASTER RIFLE

Blasters fire bursts of particle-beam energy from power cells. Standard types are internally modified for use by different soldiers (battle droids, clone troopers, stormtroopers, Rebel troops, etc.). Ion weapons fire ion energy instead of blaster bolts.

Droid Transports

Six battle droids with blasters can be deployed from the sliding droid rack on the repulsorlift carrier (set 7126). The armed repulsorlift carrier (set 7654) transports five standing droids and two blasters, with a pilot droid seated in the cockpit. The set also comes with a STAP and three super battle droids.

Set name	Battle Droid Carrier	
Year 2001	Number	7126
Pieces 133	Film	EP I

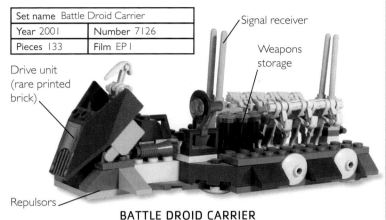

Signal receiver

Weapons storage

Drive unit (rare printed brick)

Repulsors

BATTLE DROID CARRIER

Defensive drive unit

Laser cannon

DROID TRANSPORT CARRIER

Set name	Droids Battle Pack	
Year 2007	Number	7654
Pieces 102	Film	EP III

Droideka

Destroyer droids, or droidekas, roll into battle, uncurl, encase themselves in a semi-transparent energy shield, and then deploy built-in blasters to deadly effect. The 2002 version came with the Republic Gunship (set 7163) and Jedi Defense I (set 7203). The 2007 version came with the Trade Federation MTT (set 7662).

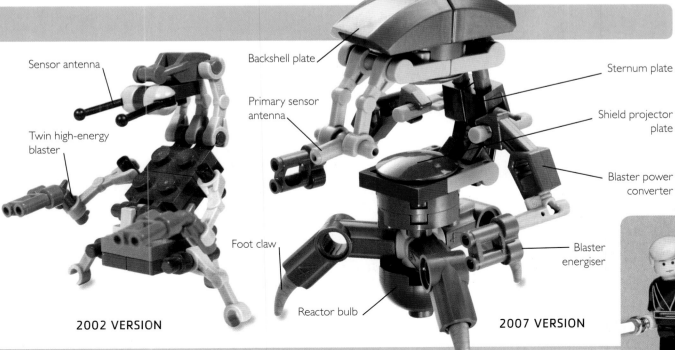

Sensor antenna

Twin high-energy blaster

2002 VERSION

Backshell plate

Primary sensor antenna

Foot claw

Reactor bulb

Sternum plate

Shield projector plate

Blaster power converter

Blaster energiser

2007 VERSION

▼ Gunship

The Republic gunship, or Low-Altitude Assault Transport/infantry (LAAT/i), deploys clone soldiers into battle. Troops dismount through sliding doors, under cover of swivelling laser cannons (two on the front and one at the back) and four laser turrets (two manned and two remote). The nose opens to reveal a magnetically held, detachable prison cell.

Republic Army

For generations, the Republic had no army, relying only on the Jedi Knights to maintain peace and justice in the galaxy. But the vast Separatist Droid Army forced Republic leaders to take decisive action. The Galactic Republic quickly amassed one of the largest armies ever seen. Its ranks are made up of clone troopers and its ground and air vehicles are diverse and specialised.

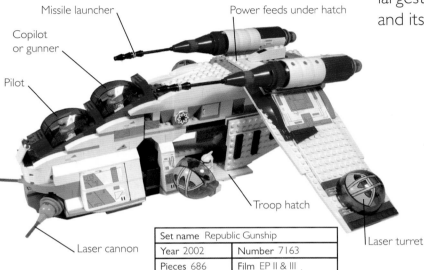

Missile launcher

Power feeds under hatch

Copilot or gunner

Pilot

Troop hatch

Laser cannon

Set name	Republic Gunship	
Year 2002	Number 7163	
Pieces 686	Film EP II & III	

Laser turret

▼ AT-TE Walker

The six-legged All Terrain Tactical Enforcer, or AT-TE walker, blasts ground or air targets with its massive cannon, while its six laser cannon turrets focus on smaller targets. This modified AT-TE carries four clones and, in the rear compartment, a speeder bike.

SPEEDER BIKE

Set name	AT-TE	
Year 2003	Number 4482	
Pieces 658	Film EP II & III	

▼ BARC Speeder

This two-person Biker Advanced Recon Commando (BARC) speeder often escorts gunships carrying important passengers. Propelled by repulsors and a turbine engine, the bike is armed with two sets of blasters on each side and a pair of ion cannons.

Cannon operated by gunner

Bar step access to cabin

Driver inside cabin

Republic emblem

Ion cannon

Pursuit blaster

Turbojet airscoop

Set name	Clone Troopers Battle Pack	
Year 2007	Number 7655	
Pieces 58	Film EP III	

Rotating mechanical leg joints

Laser cannon turret

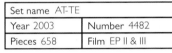

▼ V-Wing Starfighter

Clone troopers pilot agile V-wing fighters, with spherical Q7 astromechs (head only) as copilots. The wings unfold in flight and the laser cannons are powerful and deadly.

Set name	V-Wing Starfighter
Year 2006	Number 6205
Pieces 118	Film EP III

Clone pilot

Wing unfolded in flight

Spherical Q7-series astromech

Swivelling laser cannons

▷ AT-AP Walker

Rotating saddle

Elevating blaster cannon

The All Terrain Attack Pod (AT-AP) is a two-legged walker. (This version also has a third retractable stabilizer leg when used as a gun emplacement.) It is equipped with massive blaster cannons; the roof and side doors open to reveal an interior cabin.

Repeating blaster

Set name	AT-AP Walker
Year 2008	Number 7671
Pieces 392	Film EP III

Wing-mounted laser cannon

Hinged cockpit screen

Reverse articulation coupler

▷ ARC-170 Starfighter

The Aggressive ReConnaissance (ARC-170) fighter is hyperdrive-equipped for long-range missions. Its crew consists of three clones and an R4 astromech. The ship's wings unfold and splay when in flight, while a payload of mines can be dropped from the underside.

Republic red-colour styling

Set name	ARC-170 Starfighter
Year 2005	Number 7259
Pieces 396	Film EP III

R4-SERIES DROID

Heat sinks and cooling radiator panels on split wings

▼ Turbo Tank (2005)

The Clone Turbo Tank, properly called the HAV A6 Juggernaut, or more simply, the 'rolling slab', is the stuff of legend. Its armour is nearly impenetrable, its weapons are devastating and its ten wheels crush droids under them. A BARC speeder is stored inside.

BARC SPEEDER

Look-out turret

Set name	Clone Turbo Tank
Year 2005	Number 7261
Pieces 801	Film EP III

Rear cockpit hatch

▼ AT-RT Walker

The All Terrain Recon Transport (AT-RT), or scout walker, is an open-cockpit recon vehicle.

Set name	Clone Scout Walker
Year 2005	Number 7250
Pieces 108	Film EP III

Captain-rank clone trooper

Repeating blaster

Wheel suspension

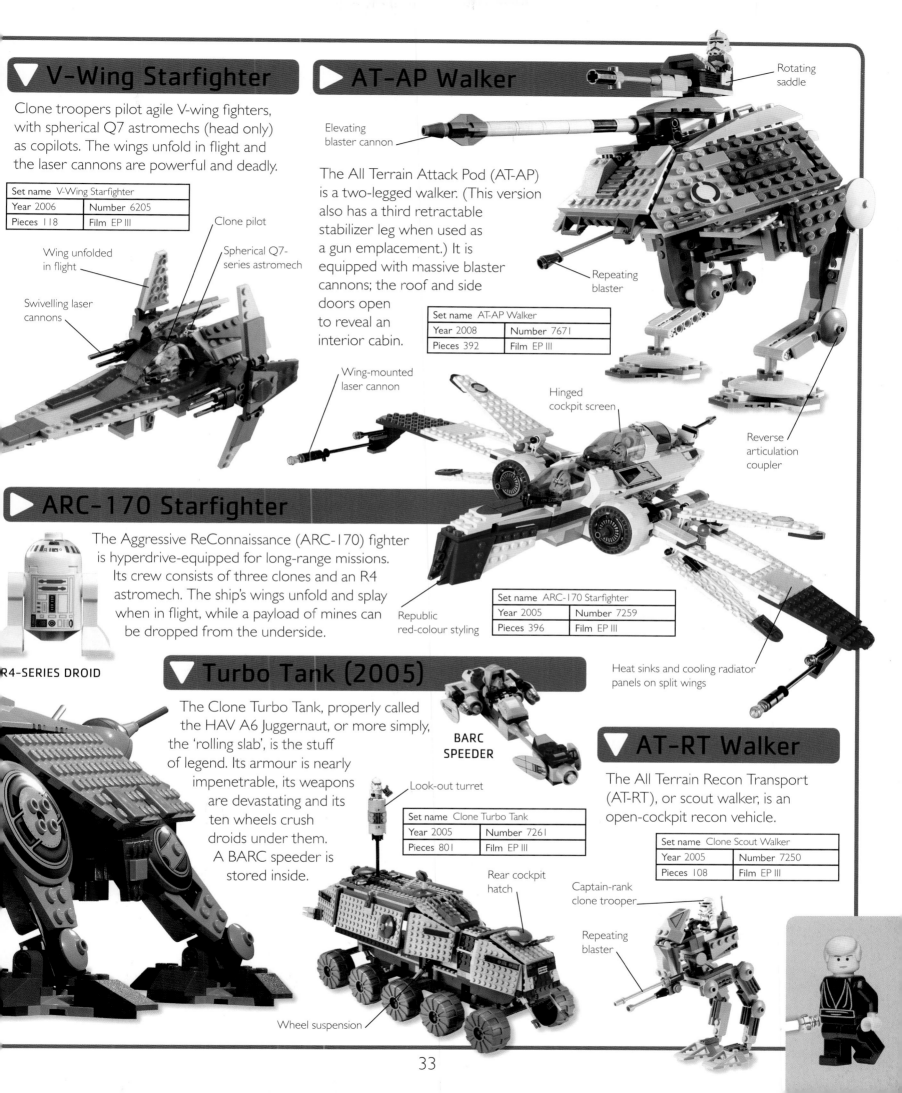

Clone Troopers

At the start of the Clone Wars, clone troopers wear Phase I armour, which is loosely based on Jango Fett's Mandalorian shock trooper armour. Informally called 'the body bucket', this armour is heavy and often uncomfortable. Coloured stripes denote rank. During the later part of the Clone Wars, Phase II armour mainly replaces Phase I armour. Phase II armour is stronger, lighter and more adaptable than the earlier type, with many specialist variations. Colour now denotes unit affiliation, not rank.

▼ Phase I Trooper

Phase I clone trooper minifigures wear basic white armour with white helmets. Under the helmets, their heads are black, without faces.

Breath filter

◀ Phase II Trooper

Episode III sets were issued with clone troopers wearing Phase II armour. Their helmets feature improved breath filter/ annunciators and their heads are plain black under the helmets. Camouflage is sometimes used on Phase II armour.

Audio pickup

Heat dispersal vents

Gas cartridge cap

Blaster power cell

Heat radiator fins

Macrobinoculars

Republic emblem

Clone pilots are trained to fly hyperdrive-capable ships including ARC-170s and V-wing starfighters. These clones wear air-supply helmets, white armour, and blue flightsuits.

Air-supply hose

Spare blaster magazine

CLONE PILOT

STAR CORPS TROOPER
Star Corps clone troopers, attached to the 327th Star Corps, are an elite force with yellow armour markings. One appears with the Clone Turbo Tank (set 7261) and the Clone Troopers Battle Pack (set 7655).

BRICK FACTS

- A slightly adapted Phase I clone trooper appears with *Star Wars*: The Clone Wars (animated TV series) sets.

- Specialist ARC troopers receive a helmet-mounted rangefinder, visor, and floodlight, a kama (a flexible, anti-blast skirt) a command pauldron, and two small DC-17 commando blasters.

CLONE RECON TROOPER

Recon trooper symbol

Clone recon troopers, with red armour markings, are specialised clones that carry out short-range reconnaissance missions for Jedi Generals and clone commanders. They often utilise BARC speeders, AT-AP walkers and AT-RT walkers.

Advanced polarised visor

Clone scout troopers are equipped with green armour for camouflage on jungle worlds. Their visors are adapted for greater visibility. A scout trooper works alongside the troops on the Clone Turbo Tank set.

CLONE SCOUT TROOPER

Coruscant designation

Red-coloured shock troopers form an elite corp, stationed on Coruscant, that reports directly to Supreme Chancellor Palpatine. Two versions have been released: One has all-white legs and the other has white legs with black in the middle. Shock troopers come with the AT-AP Walker (set 7671) and the Clone Troopers Battle Pack (set 7655).

SHOCK TROOPER

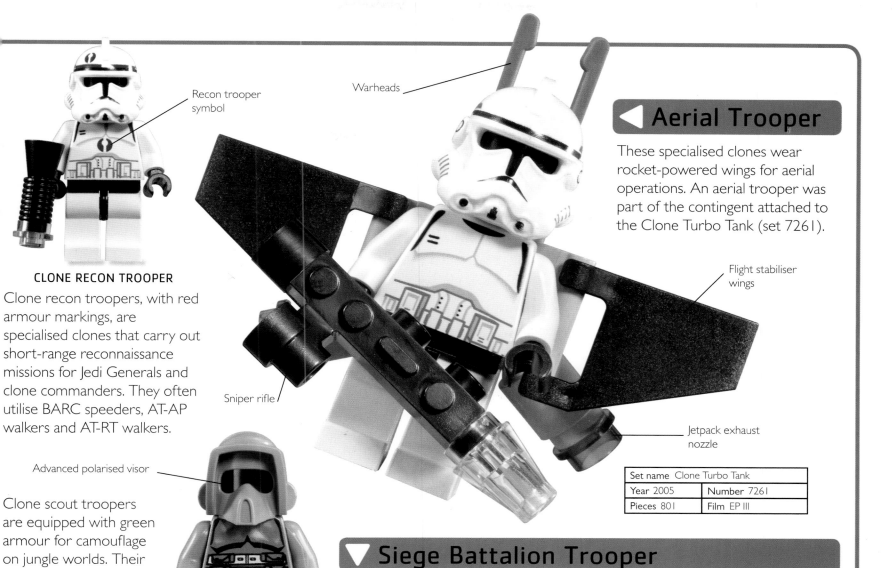

Warheads

◀ Aerial Trooper

These specialised clones wear rocket-powered wings for aerial operations. An aerial trooper was part of the contingent attached to the Clone Turbo Tank (set 7261).

Flight stabiliser wings

Sniper rifle

Jetpack exhaust nozzle

Set name	Clone Turbo Tank	
Year 2005	Number 7261	
Pieces 801	Film EP III	

▼ Siege Battalion Trooper

Two siege battalion troopers, wearing armour distinguished by green markings, pilot the ISP (Infantry Support Platform) swamp speeder that comes with the Wookiee Catamaran (set 7260).

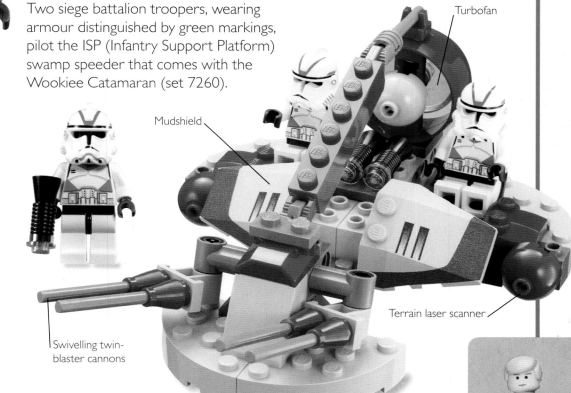

Turbofan

Mudshield

Swivelling twin-blaster cannons

Terrain laser scanner

Set name	Wookiee Catamaran	
Year 2005	Number 7260	
Pieces 376	Film EP III	

Wookiees

During the Clone Wars, an epic battle takes place on Kashyyyk, home planet of the Wookiees. Droid armies face fierce resistance from well-armed and proud Wookiee warriors, led by commander Tarfful and including Chewbacca. Wookiees use traditional wood-framed vehicles, many of which are unarmed, but the Wookiees' knowledge of the swamps and forests of their planet gives them an advantage over the ruthless droids.

On Kashyyyk, Separatist battle droids, spider droids and tanks droids launch a massive attack. The Wookiees fight bravely in their ornithopters, catamarans and other vehicles, supported by Republic clone troops led by Jedi generals.

Pressure release vents

Radiator grille

◄ **Ornithopter**

Laser cannon tail-gun

Wookiee ornithopters, also known as fluttercraft, are lightweight, two-seated fliers used to patrol the swamps of Kashyyyk. During the Battle of Kashyyyk, Wookiee pilots and gunners fly these open-cockpit craft, many retrofitted with tail-mounted laser cannons, relying on speed and agility to avoid incoming fire.

Wooden framework

Steering vanes

Manoeuvrable flight wings

Set name	Wookiee Attack	
Year 2005	Number 7258	
Pieces 366	Film EP III	

The Wookiees faced droids piloting a variety of war vehicles. This small, open-cockpit tank is fast and agile.

SWAMP SKIMMER

Power generator

SMALL ASSAULT TANK

Secondary laser blaster

This single-Wookiee Swamp Skimmer is used as a scout and patrol vehicle. Resourceful Wookiee engineers crafted it using spare parts from existing vehicles.

Dual drive treads

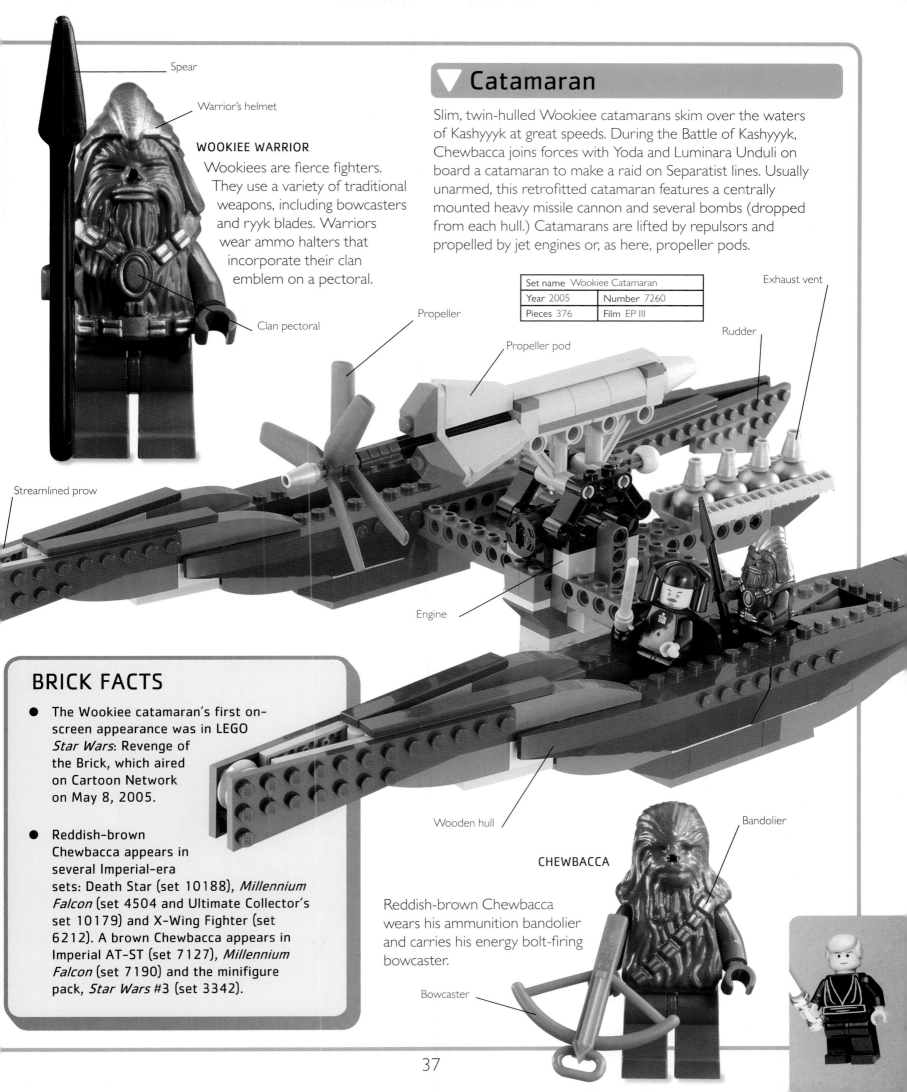

Spear

Warrior's helmet

WOOKIEE WARRIOR

Wookiees are fierce fighters. They use a variety of traditional weapons, including bowcasters and ryyk blades. Warriors wear ammo halters that incorporate their clan emblem on a pectoral.

Clan pectoral

Streamlined prow

▼ Catamaran

Slim, twin-hulled Wookiee catamarans skim over the waters of Kashyyyk at great speeds. During the Battle of Kashyyyk, Chewbacca joins forces with Yoda and Luminara Unduli on board a catamaran to make a raid on Separatist lines. Usually unarmed, this retrofitted catamaran features a centrally mounted heavy missile cannon and several bombs (dropped from each hull.) Catamarans are lifted by repulsors and propelled by jet engines or, as here, propeller pods.

Set name	Wookiee Catamaran	
Year 2005	Number	7260
Pieces 376	Film	EP III

Propeller

Propeller pod

Exhaust vent

Rudder

Engine

BRICK FACTS

● The Wookiee catamaran's first on-screen appearance was in LEGO *Star Wars*: Revenge of the Brick, which aired on Cartoon Network on May 8, 2005.

● Reddish-brown Chewbacca appears in several Imperial-era sets: Death Star (set 10188), *Millennium Falcon* (set 4504 and Ultimate Collector's set 10179) and X-Wing Fighter (set 6212). A brown Chewbacca appears in Imperial AT-ST (set 7127), *Millennium Falcon* (set 7190) and the minifigure pack, *Star Wars* #3 (set 3342).

Wooden hull

Bandolier

CHEWBACCA

Reddish-brown Chewbacca wears his ammunition bandolier and carries his energy bolt-firing bowcaster.

Bowcaster

Luke Skywalker

Yearning for adventure, farm boy Luke Skywalker grows up on a remote planet named Tatooine. When he meets Obi-Wan Kenobi, Luke begins to learn the truth of his origins as the secret son of Anakin Skywalker. Luke's journey transforms him into a Rebel pilot and a Jedi Knight – and ends in reconciliation with his father and freedom from Imperial rule for the galaxy.

▶ T-16 Skyhopper

With the demise of Podracing on Tatooine, teenagers take to racing skyhoppers through narrow ravines, blasting womp rats with front-mounted rifles. Luke owns an Incom T-16 skyhopper (though his Uncle Owen disapproves of it). This variant model features an open cockpit (standard models feature a pressurised cabin for sub-orbital travel). A compartment in the upper airfoil holds the electrobinoculars and blaster included with the set.

SKYHOPPER PILOT

Wearing a visor, red helmet and red flight overalls, this skyhopper pilot could easily be Luke Skywalker.

Upper airfoil

Pilot in open cockpit

Flying decal

Wing-mounted cannon

Heavy-duty gun

Movable lower airfoil

Set name	T-16 Skyhopper	
Year	2003	Number 4477
Pieces	96	Film EP IV

▼ Landspeeder

Luke travels around the desert terrain of his homeworld on a battered X-34 landspeeder. Its low-power repulsors make it hover off the ground, while triple turbines provide thrust.

TATOOINE LUKE

On desolate Tatooine, Luke wears a simple farm tunic, utility belt and leg bindings.

Set name	Mos Eisley Cantina	
Year	2004	Number 4501
Pieces	193	Film EP IV

Turbine jet engine

Twin seats

Secret storage compartment

Light-grey, damaged turbine engine

Duraplex windshield

Obi-Wan Kenobi

Air circulation grille

LANDSPEEDER (1999)

This tan-coloured landspeeder carries Luke and Obi-Wan.

Set name	Landspeeder	
Year	1999	Number 7110
Pieces	47	Film EP IV

X-Wing (1999)

Luke first flies an X-wing as 'Red Five' in the daring Rebel attack on the first Death Star. The ship has a hinged cockpit canopy, a droid socket for R2-D2 and four long-range laser cannons. S-foil wings lock into an x-shaped attack formation. A ground crew mechanic stands by with a utility train equipped with repair-and-maintenance tools, along with fellow Rebel pilot (and Luke's old friend) Biggs Darklighter.

Set name	X-Wing Fighter	
Year 1999	Number 7140	
Pieces 263	Film EP IV, V & VI	

Life support unit

REBEL PILOT

When Luke flies with the Rebel Alliance, he wears an orange pressurised g-suit with an insulated flying helmet.

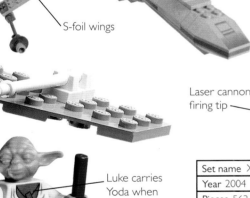

S-foil wings

Laser cannon firing tip

Luke carries Yoda when training

JEDI IN TRAINING

When Luke is training with Yoda, he wears a sleeveless green shirt, grey pants and a green backpack.

Nose cone

Set name	X-Wing Fighter	
Year 2004	Number 4502	
Pieces 563	Film EP IV, V & VI	

BRICK FACTS

● In 2009, LEGO made an exclusive Luke Skywalker minifigure for DK's *LEGO Star Wars: The Visual Dictionary*. As the book celebrates 10 years of LEGO *Star Wars*, Luke is dressed for the celebration scene at the end of *Star Wars: Episode IV A New Hope*.

CELEBRATION LUKE

X-Wing (2004)

Luke Skywalker flies his X-wing fighter to Dagobah to train as a Jedi with Yoda. Crash-landing in a bog, the ship is festooned with swamp weeds. The craft has a cockpit that opens for Luke and moveable wings which spread into 'attack' formation (operated by turning a knob that moves all four wings at once).

Cockpit canopy

Hyperdrive

Hinged, drop-down storage compartment

Engine nozzle

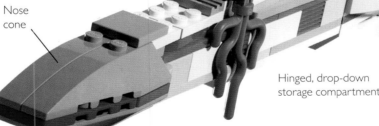

X-Wing (2006)

This X-wing features opening wings (via a turning dial in the back), functional landing gear, a hinged cockpit canopy and a cargo hold for Luke's lightsabre. It can be customised as either Luke Skywalker's Red Five or Wedge Antilles's X-wing. The set includes minifigures of Luke, Wedge, Princess Leia, Han Solo, Chewbacca and R2-D2.

Cargo hold

Lower wing

Landing gear

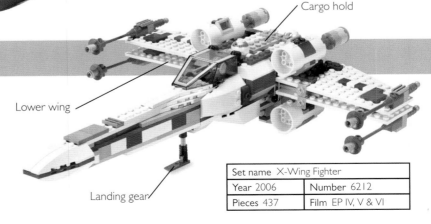

Set name	X-Wing Fighter	
Year 2006	Number 6212	
Pieces 437	Film EP IV, V & VI	

Workshop

In the workshop, Jawas use scrap parts to mend broken equipment or droids. After a sale, the Jawas move on quickly, as their patched-up goods rarely remain working for long.

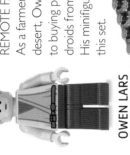

JAWA WORKSHOP

REMOTE FARMER
As a farmer living in a remote desert, Owen Lars is resigned to buying poor-quality work droids from passing Jawas. His minifigure is unique to this set.

OWEN LARS

ESCAPE POD
C-3PO and R2-D2 slip into a small escape pod to escape the clutches of Darth Vader when he captures the Rebel Blockade Runner. After the droids crash-land on Tatooine, Jawas capture them and sell them to Owen Lars.

Set name	Droid Escape	
Year 2001		Number 7106
Pieces 44		Film EP IV

Thrusters

Cockpit

A Jawa steers the sandcrawler from inside the cockpit situated high on the front of the vehicle. It is hinged at the top for access.

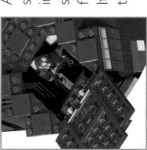

Cockpit hatch hinged for access

Roof hatch can open to transfer droids in and out

Mining support apparatus

Warning light

Reactor generator casing

Power cells

Tool rack

Repair station viewscreen

Repair station computer

Forward roof hatch (lifts out)

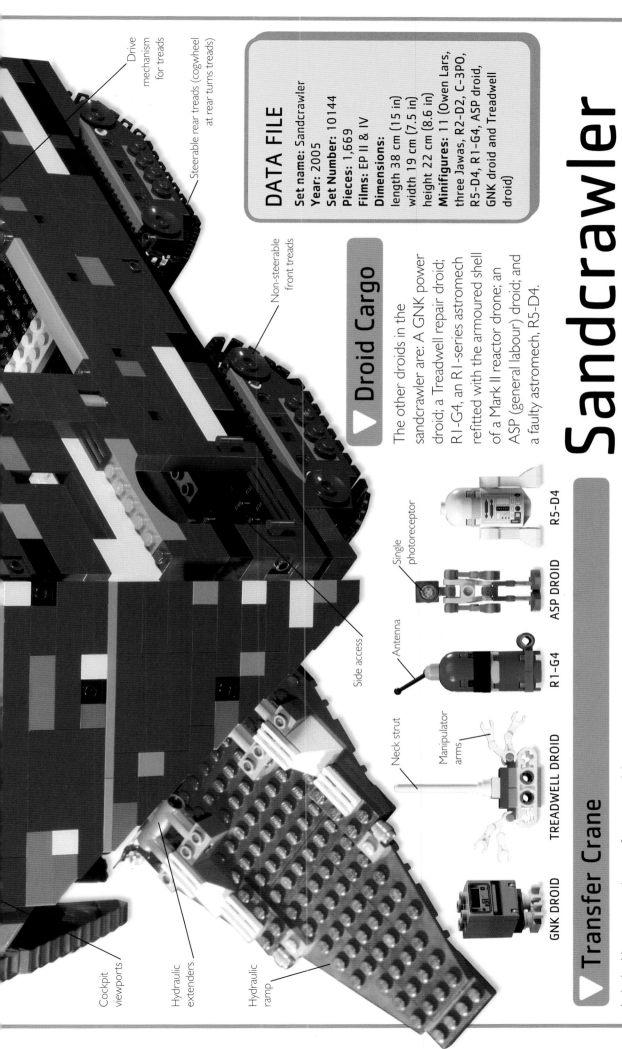

Drive mechanism for treads

Steerable rear treads (cogwheel at rear turns treads)

Non-steerable front treads

Side access

Cockpit viewports

Hydraulic extenders

Hydraulic ramp

DATA FILE

Set name: Sandcrawler
Year: 2005
Set Number: 10144
Pieces: 1,669
Films: EP II & IV
Dimensions:
length 38 cm (15 in)
width 19 cm (7.5 in)
height 22 cm (8.6 in)
Minifigures: 11 (Owen Lars, three Jawas, R2-D2, C-3PO, R5-D4, R1-G4, ASP droid, GNK droid and Treadwell droid)

▶ Droid Cargo

The other droids in the sandcrawler are: A GNK power droid; a Treadwell repair droid; R1-G4, an R1-series astromech refitted with the armoured shell of a Mark II reactor drone; an ASP (general labour) droid; and a faulty astromech, R5-D4.

Single photoreceptor

R5-D4

Antenna

ASP DROID

Neck strut

Manipulator arms

R1-G4

TREADWELL DROID

GNK DROID

Sandcrawler

On Tatooine, Jawa sandcrawlers patrol the deserts and wastelands in search of salvage from spaceship crashes. Sandcrawlers are forgotten relics from the days when Tatooine was a mining colony. Jawas have repurposed them to round up stray droids, junked vehicles, and any unwanted scrap metal or minerals that can be used or sold. Each sandcrawler is home to an entire clan of Jawas, and serves as transport, workshop, traveling store – and safe protection from desert predators or rampaging Sand People.

▶ Transfer Crane

A transfer crane picks up scrap droids and transports them into the bowels of the sandcrawler, where they are either mended or broken up for spare parts. The crane can attach to the sandcrawler roof.

Lifting arm

Winch

R2-D2 being lifted

Control lever

Ionisation blaster

Bandolier

JAWA

Han Solo and Chewbacca

▼ Cantina

When one of Jabba the Hutt's minions, Greedo, accosts Han Solo in the Mos Eisley Cantina, only one of them will leave the table. Here's a clue: Solo's blaster pistol is stored in a compartment under the table.

**HAN SOLO
(MOS EISLEY)**

Facing Greedo in the Mos Eisley Cantina, Han wears his black vest and dark blue trousers (with holster).

Set name	Mos Eisley Cantina	
Year 2004	Number 4501	
Pieces 193	Film EP IV	

Greedo

Entrance archway

He's a rogue and a scoundrel. Worst of all, according to Princess Leia, he's scruffy looking. But Han Solo and copilot Chewbacca fly one of the fastest ships in the galaxy. The *Millennium Falcon* is also scruffy looking, but, according to Solo, it "made the Kessel run in less than 12 parsecs". The ship needs to be smart and fast: Solo has a bounty on his head for unpaid debts to Jabba the Hutt. What a time to get mixed up in a Rebellion against the Empire!

▼ Millennium Falcon (2000)

This version of Han Solo's battered but trusty YT-1300 light freighter includes an escape pod (or 'scout sled') that can be jettisoned from the side. The top can be removed to reveal the navicomputer, smuggling compartments and main hold with Dejarik hologame.

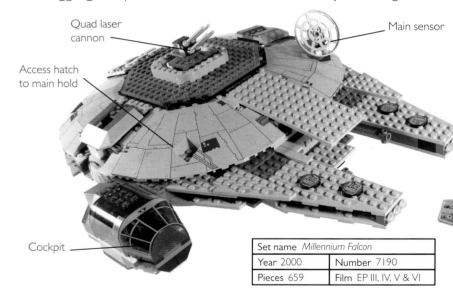

Quad laser cannon

Main sensor

Access hatch to main hold

Cockpit

Set name	Millennium Falcon	
Year 2000	Number 7190	
Pieces 659	Film EP III, IV, V & VI	

BRICK FACTS

● The *Millennium Falcon* (set 4504) reappeared in Battle of Yavin Collection (K10131) along with TIE Collection (set 10131) and X-Wing Fighter (set 4502).

● In *A New Hope*, the *Falcon* jettisoned its escape pods before being pulled into the Death Star.

Detachable pod roof

ESCAPE POD

▶ Millennium Falcon (2004)

In this set, Han Solo wears his Hoth outfit with tan-coloured trousers (with holster) and blue shirt (with printed binoculars.) In the X-Wing Fighter (set 6212, issued in 2006), Solo's trousers are red-brown.

**HAN SOLO
(HOTH)**

Set name	Millennium Falcon	
Year 2004	Number 4504	
Pieces 985	Film EP III, IV, V & VI	

After the disastrous Battle of Hoth, Han Solo and Chewbacca pilot the *Falcon* to Cloud City with Princess Leia and C-3PO on board. Hinged exterior panels reveal the main hold (with chairs and hologame) and, at the rear, the hyperdrive and engine room. Pulling on the docking port lowers the boarding ramp. A minifigure can be placed in the seat to aim and fire the upper quad laser cannon.

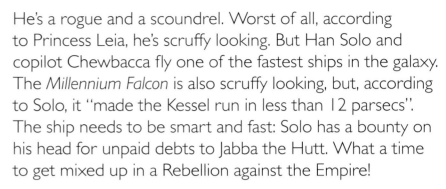

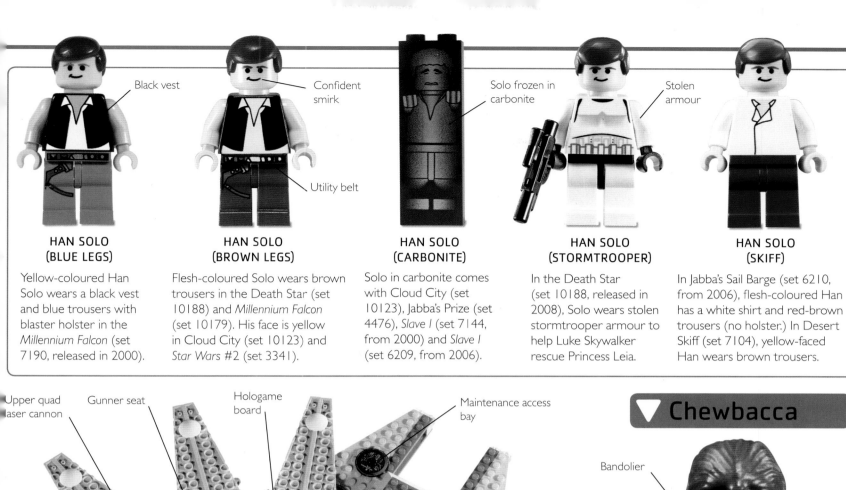

HAN SOLO (BLUE LEGS)

Yellow-coloured Han Solo wears a black vest and blue trousers with blaster holster in the *Millennium Falcon* (set 7190, released in 2000).

Black vest

Confident smirk

Utility belt

HAN SOLO (BROWN LEGS)

Flesh-coloured Solo wears brown trousers in the Death Star (set 10188) and *Millennium Falcon* (set 10179). His face is yellow in Cloud City (set 10123) and *Star Wars* #2 (set 3341).

Solo frozen in carbonite

HAN SOLO (CARBONITE)

Solo in carbonite comes with Cloud City (set 10123), Jabba's Prize (set 4476), *Slave I* (set 7144, from 2000) and *Slave I* (set 6209, from 2006).

Stolen armour

HAN SOLO (STORMTROOPER)

In the Death Star (set 10188, released in 2008), Solo wears stolen stormtrooper armour to help Luke Skywalker rescue Princess Leia.

HAN SOLO (SKIFF)

In Jabba's Sail Barge (set 6210, from 2006), flesh-coloured Han has a white shirt and red-brown trousers (no holster.) In Desert Skiff (set 7104), yellow-faced Han wears brown trousers.

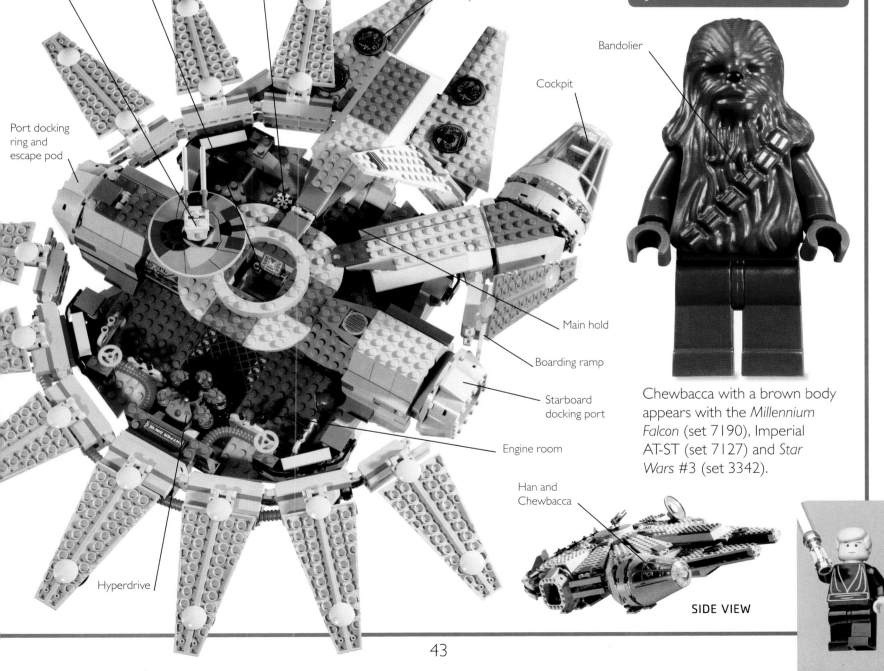

Upper quad laser cannon

Gunner seat

Hologame board

Maintenance access bay

Port docking ring and escape pod

Hyperdrive

Main hold

Boarding ramp

Starboard docking port

Engine room

▼ Chewbacca

Bandolier

Cockpit

Chewbacca with a brown body appears with the *Millennium Falcon* (set 7190), Imperial AT-ST (set 7127) and *Star Wars* #3 (set 3342).

Han and Chewbacca

SIDE VIEW

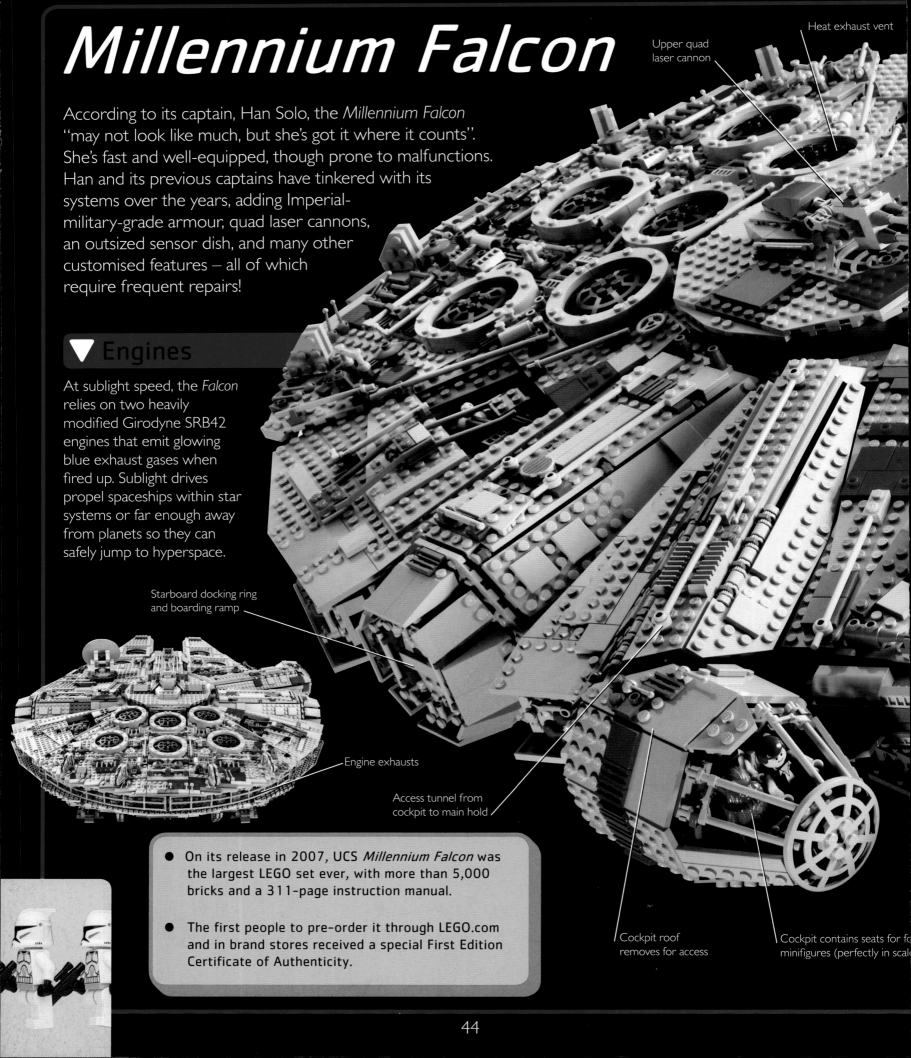

Millennium Falcon

Upper quad
laser cannon

Heat exhaust vent

According to its captain, Han Solo, the *Millennium Falcon*
"may not look like much, but she's got it where it counts".
She's fast and well-equipped, though prone to malfunctions.
Han and its previous captains have tinkered with its
systems over the years, adding Imperial-
military-grade armour, quad laser cannons,
an outsized sensor dish, and many other
customised features – all of which
require frequent repairs!

▼ Engines

At sublight speed, the *Falcon*
relies on two heavily
modified Girodyne SRB42
engines that emit glowing
blue exhaust gases when
fired up. Sublight drives
propel spaceships within star
systems or far enough away
from planets so they can
safely jump to hyperspace.

Starboard docking ring
and boarding ramp

Engine exhausts

Access tunnel from
cockpit to main hold

Cockpit roof
removes for access

Cockpit contains seats for fo
minifigures (perfectly in scal

- On its release in 2007, UCS *Millennium Falcon* was
  the largest LEGO set ever, with more than 5,000
  bricks and a 311-page instruction manual.

- The first people to pre-order it through LEGO.com
  and in brand stores received a special First Edition
  Certificate of Authenticity.

Main sensor dish elevates and rotates

▼ Quad laser cannons

A minifigure can sit in the gunner's seat facing upward to operate the upper quad laser cannons, which rotate for aiming and firing. The lower quad laser cannons can also rotate on their turrets.

Luke in gunner's seat

Maintenance access bay

Armour plate

Freight loading room

Front mandibles used in cargo transport using extendible freight loading arms

Forward floodlight

The *Falcon*'s crew enter via a retractable boarding ramp that lowers from behind the starboard docking ring. When in danger, Han can't get inside there fast enough!

DATA FILE

Set name: *Millennium Falcon*
Year: 2007   **Set Number:** 10179
Pieces: 5,195   **Films:** IV, V & VI
Dimensions:
Length 84 cm (33 in)
Width 56 cm (22 in)
Height 21 cm (8.3 in)
Minifigures: 5 (Han Solo, Chewbacca, Luke Skywalker, Obi-Wan Kenobi and Princess Leia Organa)

Imperial Shuttle

The *Lambda*-class shuttle is a multi-purpose transport vessel used throughout the Imperial fleet. These unusually elegant vessels also carry the Imperial elite, including Emperor Palpatine and Darth Vader. It is an ominous sight when the yellow-faced Palpatine minifigure, grasping his superfluous cane and flanked by red-robed Imperial guards, appears from the shuttle, piloted by an Imperial shuttle pilot.

Emperor Palpatine

Feared Sith Lord Emperor Palpatine rules as dictator over the most oppressive regime the galaxy has ever known. Rarely seen, even by his own officers, the Emperor wears a black hood over a face that has been deformed by dark side energies. Never content with the extent of his rule, Emperor Palpatine's focus now is on replacing his apprentice, Darth Vader, with Vader's own son, the powerful Jedi Luke Skywalker.

Emperor Palpatine

Emperor Palpatine's face is distorted by Dark Side energies and his sulphurous eyes betray his inner anger. Palpatine wears a black robe to hide his face and often walks with a cane, not because he needs it, but because he wishes to pretend that he is weak.

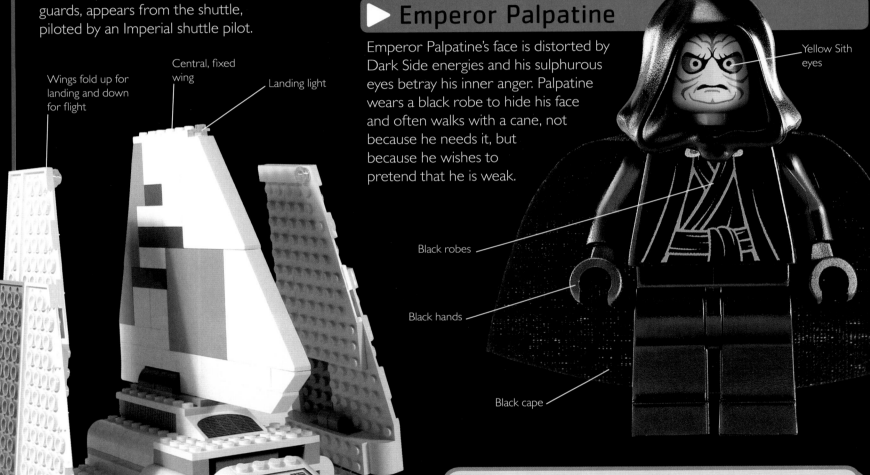

Wings fold up for landing and down for flight

Central, fixed wing

Landing light

Hyperdrive-equipped engine

Targeting sensors

Cockpit

Yellow Sith eyes

Black robes

Black hands

Black cape

Set name	Imperial Shuttle	
Year	2001	Number 7166
Pieces	234	Film EP III, IV, V & VI

BRICK FACTS

- Palpatine with a yellow face appears in Final Duel I (set 7200), Imperial Shuttle (set 7166), and the Sith Minifigure Pack (set 3340). In the Imperial Inspection (set 7264), his face and hands are grey. In the Death Star (set 10188), his face is grey and his hands are black.

- The Imperial Star Destroyer (set 6211, released in 2006) included Emperor Palpatine as a hologram.

HOLOGRAM

▼ Imperial Inspection

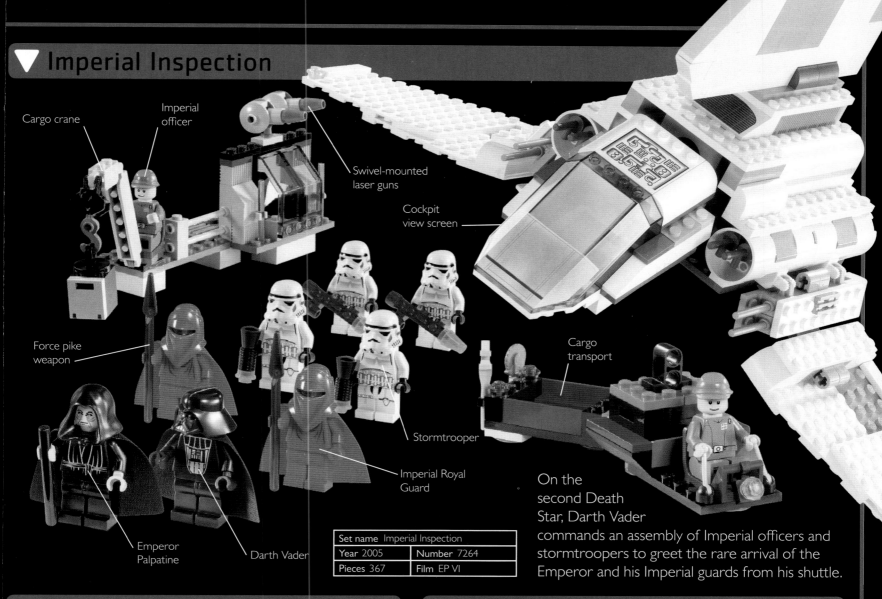

Cargo crane

Imperial officer

Swivel-mounted laser guns

Cockpit view screen

Force pike weapon

Cargo transport

Stormtrooper

Imperial Royal Guard

Emperor Palpatine

Darth Vader

Set name	Imperial Inspection	
Year	2005	Number 7264
Pieces	367	Film EP VI

On the second Death Star, Darth Vader commands an assembly of Imperial officers and stormtroopers to greet the rare arrival of the Emperor and his Imperial guards from his shuttle.

▼ Surrender on Endor

On the Imperial landing platform on Endor, a stormtrooper and an Imperial Officer (who is clearly enjoying the task) escorts Luke Skywalker to Darth Vader. Together, they will travel to the second Death Star, where the Emperor awaits....

Set name	Final Duel II	
Year	2002	Number 7201
Pieces	23	Film EP VI

Doorway

Luke Skywalker

Imperial officer

Luke's lightsabre

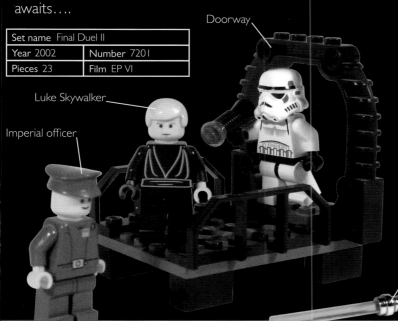

▼ Throne Room

On board the second Death Star, the Emperor commands the stars from his throne-room tower. It is here that Darth Vader steps in to save his son from the deadly Force-lightning that the Emperor lashes out at Luke Skywalker.

Swivel-mount throne

Vader with red-bladed lightsabre

Transparisteel viewport

Emperor's cane

Set name	Final Duel I	
Year	2002	Number 7200
Pieces	29	Film EP VI

▼ Rehabilitation Centre

After his battle with Obi-Wan Kenobi on Mustafar, Vader would have died had Palpatine not taken him to a secret medcentre on Coruscant. A medical droid stabilises Vader's burned body and organs, then encases him in a life-supporting black suit of armour.

Set name Darth Vader Transformation	
Year 2005	Number 7251
Pieces 53	Film EP III

Operating table rotates, with burned Vader on one side and reconstructed Vader on the other.

Darth Vader without cape

Medical data bank processors

Rotating tools ring

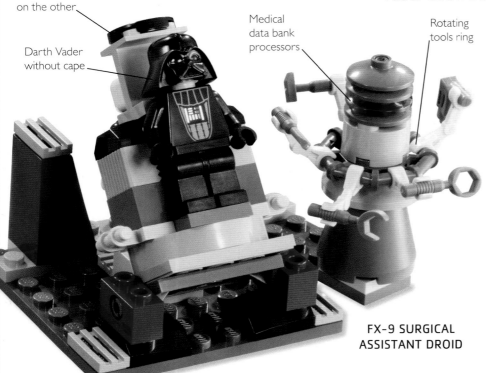

FX-9 SURGICAL ASSISTANT DROID

Darth Vader

One of the most decisive moments during the Clone Wars occurs when one of the most powerful Jedi in history, Anakin Skywalker, becomes Darth Sidious's new apprentice. Sidious renames Anakin as Darth Vader, whose first mission is to destroy the Jedi Order. Only a few Jedi escape the 'Great Jedi Purge'. Vader soon becomes a feared leader of the Empire.

▼ Darth Vader

Vader with cloak and scarred face appears in Cloud City (set 10123), Final Duel I (set 7200), TIE Fighter & Y-Wing (set 7150), and Sith Minifigure Pack (set 3340). He has more detailed chest controls and a utility belt in Darth Vader's TIE Fighter (set 8017) and Death Star (set 10188). Vader's face has no eyebrows in Imperial Inspection (set 7264) and Star Destroyer (set 6211). In TIE Fighter (set 7263), his lightsabre lights up.

Sith lightsabre with red blade

Helmet encases scarred head

Control function panel

▼ TIE Advanced (1999)

When Rebel starfighters attack the first Death Star, Darth Vader gives chase in his TIE Advanced X1 prototype – a more capable ship than the standard TIE fighter, with shields and a hyperdrive. Vader's minifigure sits in the cockpit to attack the Y-wing included in the set.

Set name TIE Fighter & Y-Wing	
Year 1999	Number 7150
Pieces 407	Film EP IV

Access hatch

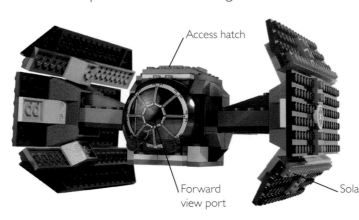

Forward view port

Solar cell wing

BRICK FACTS

- TIE Fighter & Y-Wing (set 7150) was re-released in 2002 (as set 7152).

- *Rogue Shadow* didn't appear in the movies. It was featured in the *Star Wars*: The Force Unleashed videogame.

- In 2009, a chrome Vader minifigure was inserted randomly in 10,000 sets in the US to celebrate the 10th anniversary of LEGO® *Star Wars*™.

▼ TIE Advanced (2008)

This version of Darth Vader's TIE Advanced comes with the added features of black and grey styling, flick missiles (operated by a trigger mechanism), a larger cockpit, and storage for Vader's lightsabre.

Set name	Darth Vader's TIE Fighter	
Year	2008	Number 8017
Pieces	251	Film EP IV

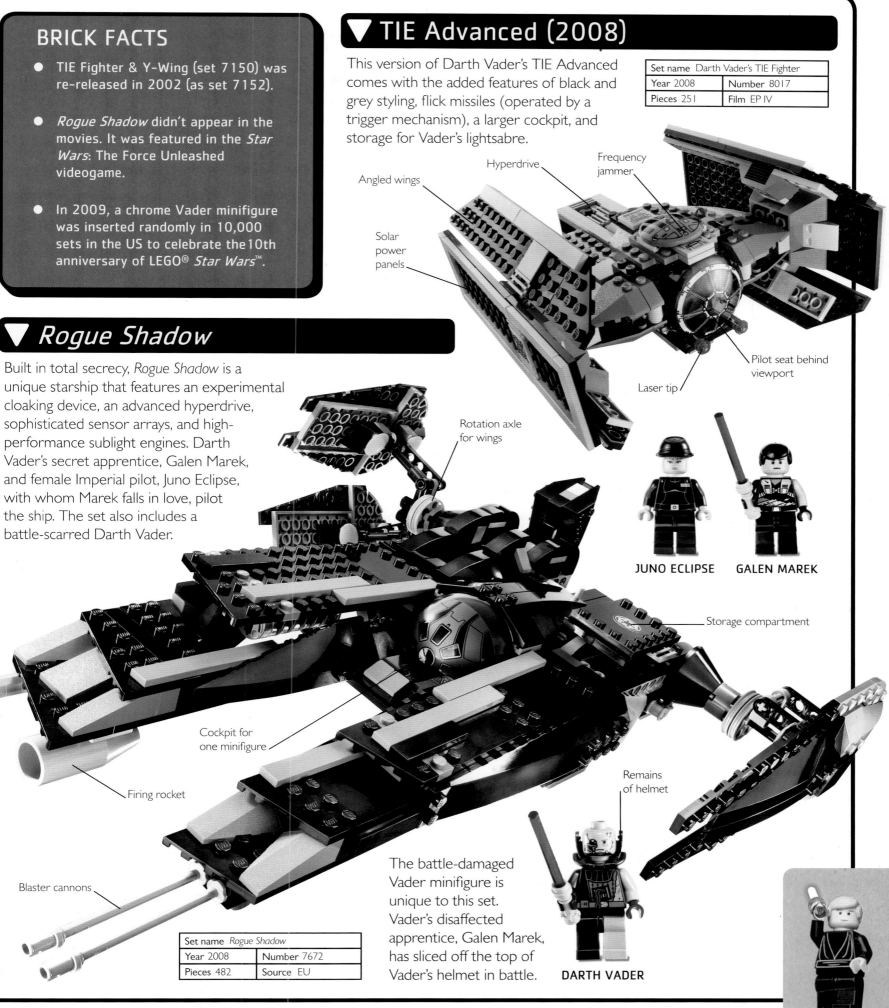

Hyperdrive

Frequency jammer

Angled wings

Solar power panels

Pilot seat behind viewport

Laser tip

▼ *Rogue Shadow*

Built in total secrecy, *Rogue Shadow* is a unique starship that features an experimental cloaking device, an advanced hyperdrive, sophisticated sensor arrays, and high-performance sublight engines. Darth Vader's secret apprentice, Galen Marek, and female Imperial pilot, Juno Eclipse, with whom Marek falls in love, pilot the ship. The set also includes a battle-scarred Darth Vader.

Rotation axle for wings

JUNO ECLIPSE

GALEN MAREK

Storage compartment

Cockpit for one minifigure

Remains of helmet

Firing rocket

Blaster cannons

The battle-damaged Vader minifigure is unique to this set. Vader's disaffected apprentice, Galen Marek, has sliced off the top of Vader's helmet in battle.

DARTH VADER

Set name	*Rogue Shadow*	
Year	2008	Number 7672
Pieces	482	Source EU

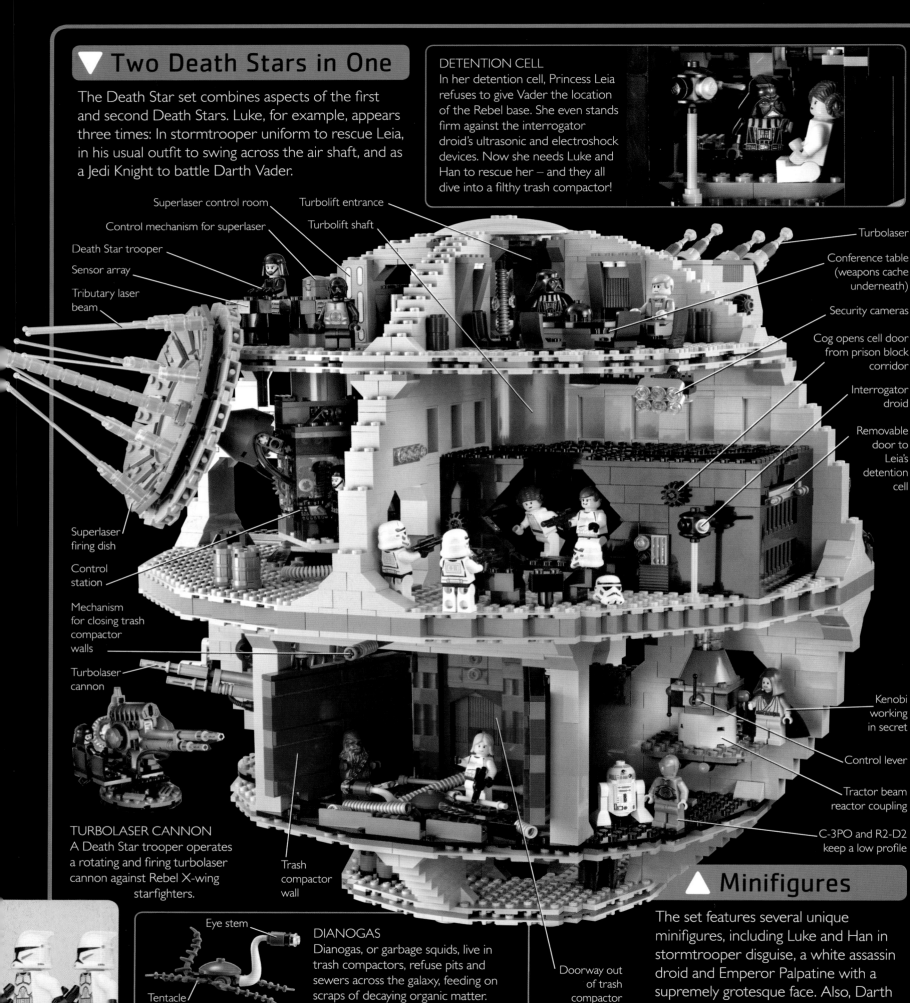

▼ Two Death Stars in One

The Death Star set combines aspects of the first and second Death Stars. Luke, for example, appears three times: In stormtrooper uniform to rescue Leia, in his usual outfit to swing across the air shaft, and as a Jedi Knight to battle Darth Vader.

DETENTION CELL
In her detention cell, Princess Leia refuses to give Vader the location of the Rebel base. She even stands firm against the interrogator droid's ultrasonic and electroshock devices. Now she needs Luke and Han to rescue her – and they all dive into a filthy trash compactor!

Superlaser control room

Control mechanism for superlaser

Death Star trooper

Sensor array

Tributary laser beam

Turbolift entrance

Turbolift shaft

Turbolaser

Conference table (weapons cache underneath)

Security cameras

Cog opens cell door from prison block corridor

Interrogator droid

Removable door to Leia's detention cell

Superlaser firing dish

Control station

Mechanism for closing trash compactor walls

Turbolaser cannon

Kenobi working in secret

Control lever

Tractor beam reactor coupling

C-3PO and R2-D2 keep a low profile

TURBOLASER CANNON
A Death Star trooper operates a rotating and firing turbolaser cannon against Rebel X-wing starfighters.

Trash compactor wall

Eye stem

DIANOGAS
Dianogas, or garbage squids, live in trash compactors, refuse pits and sewers across the galaxy, feeding on scraps of decaying organic matter.

Tentacle

Doorway out of trash compactor

▲ Minifigures

The set features several unique minifigures, including Luke and Han in stormtrooper disguise, a white assassin droid and Emperor Palpatine with a supremely grotesque face. Also, Darth Vader features a new torso design.

Death Star

The Imperial battle station known as the Death Star is designed to quash potential dissent through displays of terrifying force. The first Death Star uses its superweapon to obliterate Princess Leia's home planet Alderaan. The second Death Star, though seemingly incomplete, is actually fully operational — and is intended to lure the Rebels to their doom.

TIE ADVANCED
The mini-sized TIE Advanced is unique to the set. It can be flown into the hangar and docked on a slide-out TIE fighter rack. The cockpit viewscreen opens to allow Vader to take the controls.

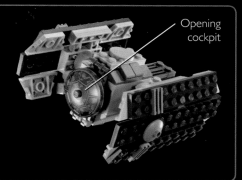

Opening cockpit

Rotating turbolaser turret

Turbolaser turning mechanism

Emperor Palpatine's throne

Guard post

Collapsing catwalk

Vader duels with Luke

Railing

Air duct

Stormtroopers on extendible bridge

Air shaft

Mechanism controls central turbolift

Rogue assassin droid

Protocol droid on work bench

Tool rack

TIE docking rack

TIE Advanced

Grand Moff Tarkin

Elevator well

Winch handle raises and lowers pilot lift

Loading bay

Cargo crane

Cargo crate

R2-Q5

Luke and Leia prepare to swing across chasm

Storage bay

Central turbolift shaft

DATA FILE

Set name: Death Star
Year: 2008
Set Number: 10188
Pieces: 3,803
Films: EP IV & VI
Dimensions: length 42 cm (16.5 in); width 42 cm (16.5 in); height 41 cm (16 in)
Minifigures: 24 – Luke Skywalker (in regular outfit, stormtrooper outfit and Jedi Knight outfit), Han Solo (regular outfit and stormtrooper outfit), Obi-Wan Kenobi, C-3PO, R2-D2, Princess Leia, Chewbacca, Darth Vader, Grand Moff Tarkin, Emperor Palpatine, 2 stormtroopers, 2 Imperial guards, assassin droid, interrogation droid, Death Star droid, 2 Death Star troopers, R2-Q5 and mouse droid.

VIEWSCREEN DISPLAYS

A viewscreen in the superlaser control room displays tracking monitor readouts of Alderaan and the Fourth Moon of Yavin as it emerges from behind the planet itself into firing range.

Imperial Army

At the end of the Clone Wars, the Galactic Republic becomes an Empire and its military resources now serve the new regime. Clone troopers become stormtroopers, their ranks made up of clones and, now, human recruits. Specialist stormtroopers are trained for a variety of military roles on land and in space.

▷ Motorised AT-AT Walker

The battery-powered motorised AT-AT can walk forwards and backwards. It features rotating laser cannons and an opening cockpit housing minifigures of General Veers, an AT-AT driver and a snowtrooper. Luke Skywalker, wearing his orange Rebel pilot flightsuit, can attach his grappling line to the underside.

Set name	Motorized Walking AT-AT	
Year 2007	Number 10178	
Pieces 1,137	Film EP V	

GENERAL VEERS

General Veers masterminds the devastating assault on the Rebel base on Hoth from the cockpit of the lead AT-AT.

Blaster cannon

SNOWTROOPER

Imperial snowtroopers wear insulated armour and a helmet with inbuilt snow goggles.

Toe flap

Luke uses harpoon gun cable to plant land mine inside AT-AT

Joint cover

Knee joint

▷ AT-AT Walker

During the Battle of Hoth, the Empire deploys All Terrain Armoured Transports (AT-ATs) against the Rebels, knowing the mere sight of these walking tanks is enough to terrify most soldiers. An AT-AT's side opens to reveal a staging platform for the two snowtrooper minifigures and its rear opens to deploy a speeder bike. An AT-AT driver steers the walker from a cockpit in its head.

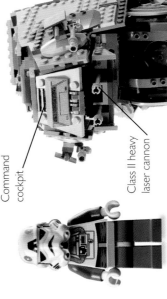

Command cockpit

Class II heavy laser cannon

AT-AT DRIVER

Equipped with insulated jumpsuits and life-support packs, AT-AT drivers guide the huge walkers.

Set name	AT-AT	
Year 2003	Number 4483	
Pieces 1,065	Film EP V	

Footpad

Speeder Bike

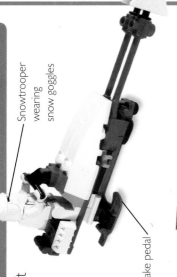

Snowtrooper wearing snow goggles

Brake pedal

AT-ATs carry high-speed repulsorlift speeder bikes for antipersonnel or reconnaissance missions. They are deployed from a garage in the rear of the AT-AT body.

Set name AT-AT	
Year 2003	Number 4483
Pieces 1,065	Film EP V

Stormtrooper

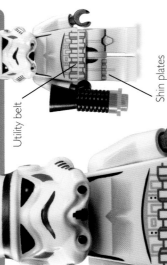

Utility belt

Shin plates

Nameless, faceless stormtroopers are utterly loyal to the Empire. Minifigures appear either with or without mouth grilles ('dotted mouths'), and with black, yellow, or flesh-coloured heads under their helmets. Stormtroopers with Imperial Inspection (set 7264) have armour shin plates.

Sandtrooper

On Tatooine, an Imperial Sandtrooper with shoulder pauldron and backpack rebreather makes a search patrol on a dewback. Unlike some Imperial vehicles, these native lizards are not immobilised by sandstorms!

Thick hide

Electro pike

Set name Mos Eisley Cantina	
Year 2004	Number 4501
Pieces 193	Film EP IV

Biker Scout

Scout troopers ride repulsorlift speeder bikes and are equipped for long-range missions without support.

Air intake

2009

AT-ST

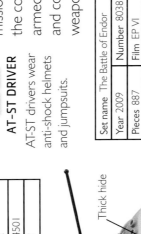

Polarized visor

AT-ST DRIVER
AT-ST drivers wear anti-shock helmets and jumpsuits.

Imperial All Terrain Scout Transports (AT-ST) can run through rugged terrain on antipersonnel or reconnaissance missions. They are piloted from the cockpit in the head and are armed with blaster and concussion weapons.

Cockpit hatch

In the 2009 set, Chewbacca appears in the stolen AT-AT at the Battle of Endor.

2009

Set name The Battle of Endor	
Year 2009	Number 8038
Pieces 887	Film EP VI

The 1999 speeder bikes also came with an Endor tree and Luke Skywalker.

1999

Set name Speeder Bikes	
Year 1999	Number 7128
Pieces 90	Film EP VI

Set name The Battle of Endor	
Year 2009	Number 8038
Pieces 887	Film EP VI

The 2001 model features Chewbacca, while the 2007 model has an Imperial pilot.

2001

Blaster cannons

2007

Set name AT-ST	
Year 2007	Number 7657
Pieces 244	Film EP V & VI

Set name Imperial AT-ST	
Year 2001	Number 7127
Pieces 107	Film EP V & VI

E-Web Blaster

At the Battle of Hoth, snowtroopers use E-Web repeating blasters on tripods.

Targeting grips

Flashback suppressor

Set name Echo Base	
Year 2009	Number 7749
Pieces 155	Film EP V

2009

Imperial Navy

When Palpatine establishes his tyrannical Empire, the Republic's massive navy is appropriated and put to brutal use. Jedi-piloted Interceptor starfighters, with their solar-panel wings, are reborn as aggressive TIE fighters. Indeed, the Imperial fleet is expanded with a variety of new, ever-deadlier models, while Emperor Palpatine travels in an updated version of the shuttle he used as Supreme Chancellor.

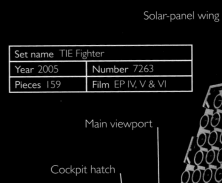

Set name	TIE Fighter	
Year 2005	Number 7263	
Pieces 159	Film EP IV, V & VI	

Solar-panel wing

Main viewport

Cockpit hatch

Laser tip

Support frame

TIE FIGHTER (2005)

▶ TIE Fighter

Swarms of deadly TIE fighters patrol the Empire, piloted by highly trained black-suited pilots. The ships are armed with laser blasters and have no deflector shields or hyperdrive, making them light and agile in battle. Set 7146 (2001) comes with a pilot, a stormtrooper and a servicing and refueling rack (which doubles as a display stand). Set 7263 (2005) stands by itself on its wings and includes a TIE pilot and Darth Vader with a light-up lightsabre.

Set name	TIE Fighter	
Year 2001	Number 7146	
Pieces 169	Film EP IV, V & VI	

Energy collection array

TIE FIGHTER (2001)

▼ Dropship

Dropships are lightly armed troop transports. A shadowtrooper sits in the cockpit and the detachable troop platform seats four stormtroopers (the set has three).

Set name	Imperial Dropship	
Year 2008	Number 7667	
Pieces 81	Film EU	

Blaster rack

Shadowtrooper in cockpit

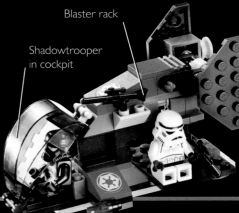

▶ Landing Craft

Like *Lambda*-class shuttles, *Sentinel*-class landing craft have a fixed central wing and two side wings that fold up when landing. They carry detachments of stormtroopers throughout the galaxy (the set comes with two stormtroopers and two sandtroopers). Piloted by an Imperial pilot, the ship boasts laser cannons, firing rockets, and four concussion missiles (released by pressing bricks in the rear).

Hinged cockpit

Laser cannon

Gear system operates wings

Set name	Imperial Landing Craft	
Year 2007	Number 7659	
Pieces 471	Film EP IV	

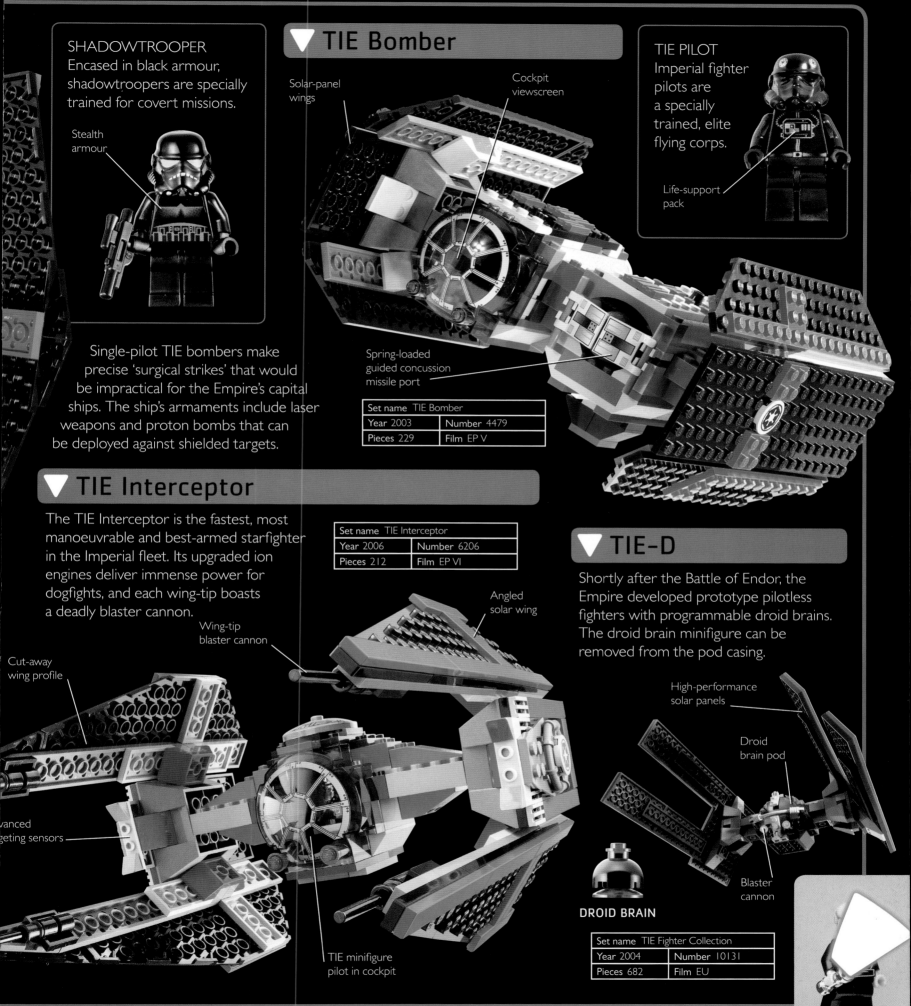

SHADOWTROOPER
Encased in black armour, shadowtroopers are specially trained for covert missions.

Stealth armour

▼ TIE Bomber

Solar-panel wings

Cockpit viewscreen

TIE PILOT
Imperial fighter pilots are a specially trained, elite flying corps.

Life-support pack

Single-pilot TIE bombers make precise 'surgical strikes' that would be impractical for the Empire's capital ships. The ship's armaments include laser weapons and proton bombs that can be deployed against shielded targets.

Spring-loaded guided concussion missile port

Set name	TIE Bomber	
Year 2003	Number 4479	
Pieces 229	Film EP V	

▼ TIE Interceptor

The TIE Interceptor is the fastest, most manoeuvrable and best-armed starfighter in the Imperial fleet. Its upgraded ion engines deliver immense power for dogfights, and each wing-tip boasts a deadly blaster cannon.

Wing-tip blaster cannon

Cut-away wing profile

Set name	TIE Interceptor	
Year 2006	Number 6206	
Pieces 212	Film EP VI	

Angled solar wing

▼ TIE-D

Shortly after the Battle of Endor, the Empire developed prototype pilotless fighters with programmable droid brains. The droid brain minifigure can be removed from the pod casing.

High-performance solar panels

Droid brain pod

vanced geting sensors

Blaster cannon

DROID BRAIN

TIE minifigure pilot in cockpit

Set name	TIE Fighter Collection	
Year 2004	Number 10131	
Pieces 682	Film EU	

Star Destroyer

Dagger-shaped Star Destroyers are the most feared symbol of Imperial might, armed with deadly firepower and powerful scanner and tractor-beam arrays. The Republic develops *Victory*-class Star Destroyers as capital ships in the final years of the Clone Wars, and the Emperor expands the fleet with new *Imperial*-class Star Destroyers, employed to crush and subdue worlds.

▼ Imperial Crew

On board the ship, Darth Vader reports to the Emperor via hologram transmission; Grand Moff Tarkin and an Imperial officer are also on board. A security force of two stormtroopers and two red-robed Imperial Royal Guards controls access areas, while droids provide support.

DARTH VADER

GRAND MOFF TARKIN

IMPERIAL OFFICER

MSE-6 DROID

STORMTROOPER

IMPERIAL GUARD

R2-Q5

▶ Forward Systems

A Star Destroyer's nose contains powerful pursuit tractor beams. The model contains a mechanism that, when pulled, ejects the escape pod through a hatch in the ship's underside.

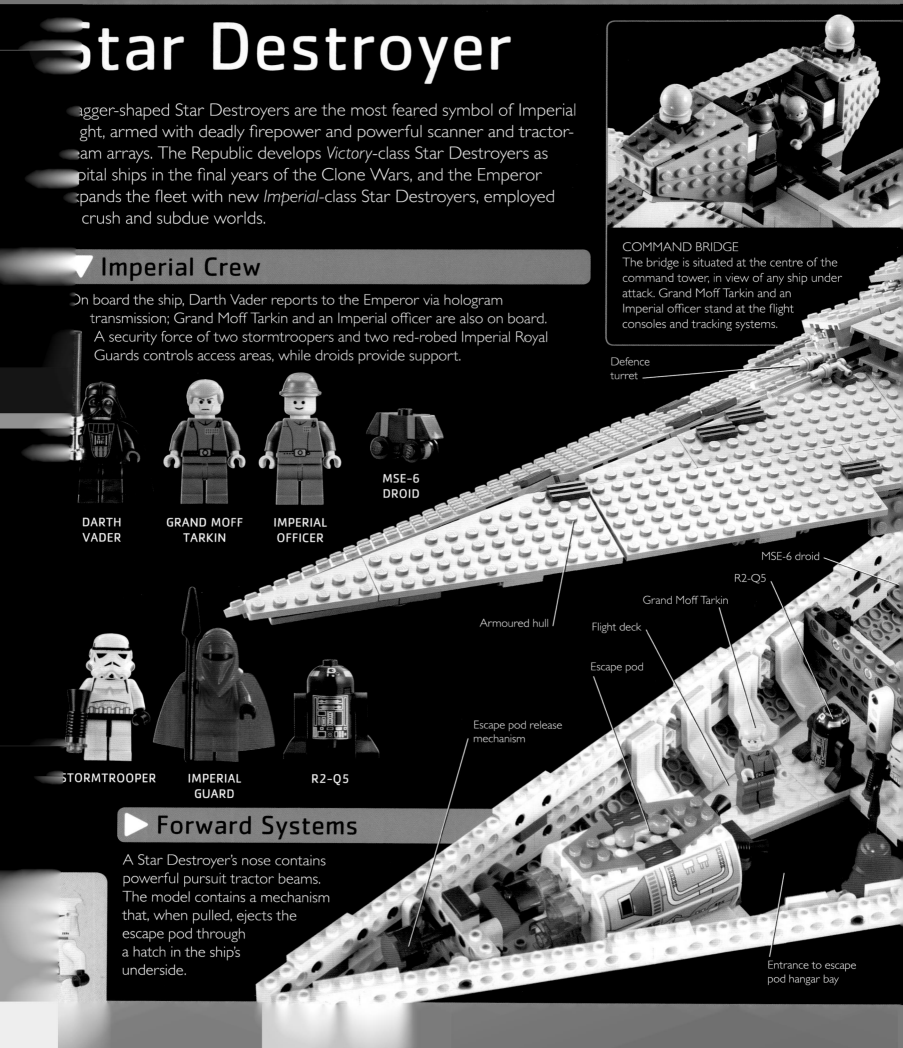

COMMAND BRIDGE
The bridge is situated at the centre of the command tower, in view of any ship under attack. Grand Moff Tarkin and an Imperial officer stand at the flight consoles and tracking systems.

Defence turret

Armoured hull

MSE-6 droid

R2-Q5

Grand Moff Tarkin

Flight deck

Escape pod

Escape pod release mechanism

Entrance to escape pod hangar bay

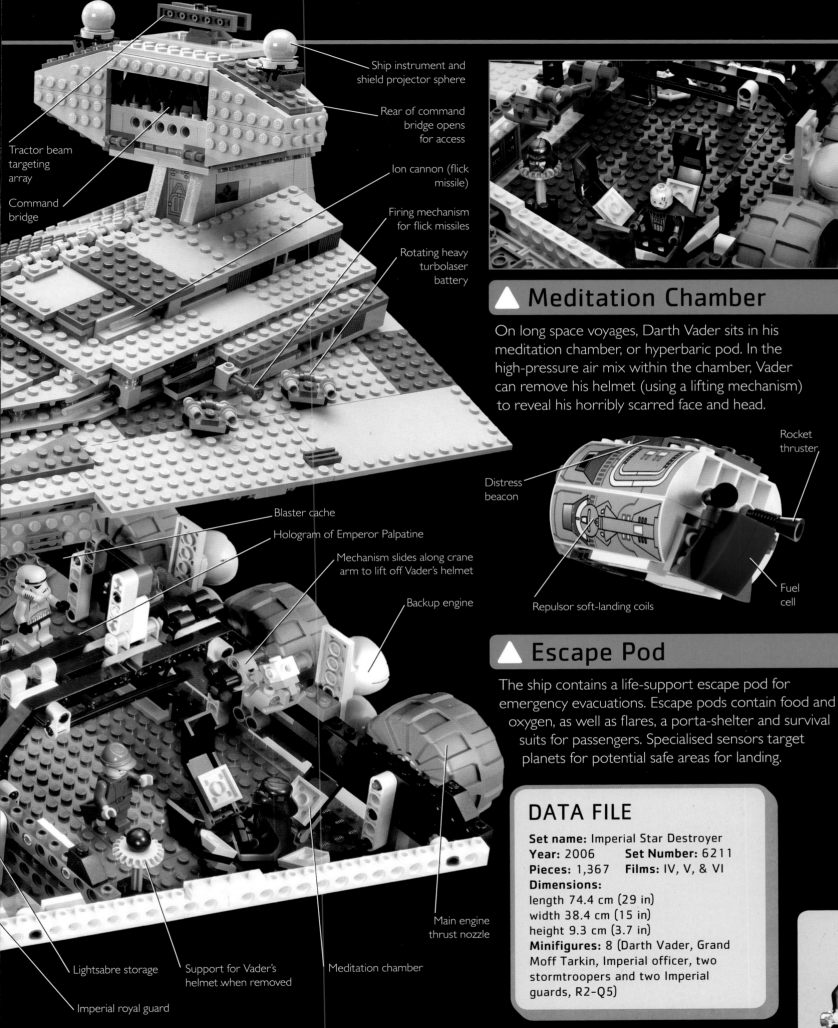

Ship instrument and shield projector sphere

Rear of command bridge opens for access

Tractor beam targeting array

Command bridge

Ion cannon (flick missile)

Firing mechanism for flick missiles

Rotating heavy turbolaser battery

Blaster cache

Hologram of Emperor Palpatine

Mechanism slides along crane arm to lift off Vader's helmet

Backup engine

Lightsabre storage

Support for Vader's helmet when removed

Meditation chamber

Main engine thrust nozzle

Imperial royal guard

▲ Meditation Chamber

On long space voyages, Darth Vader sits in his meditation chamber, or hyperbaric pod. In the high-pressure air mix within the chamber, Vader can remove his helmet (using a lifting mechanism) to reveal his horribly scarred face and head.

Rocket thruster

Distress beacon

Fuel cell

Repulsor soft-landing coils

▲ Escape Pod

The ship contains a life-support escape pod for emergency evacuations. Escape pods contain food and oxygen, as well as flares, a porta-shelter and survival suits for passengers. Specialised sensors target planets for potential safe areas for landing.

DATA FILE

Set name: Imperial Star Destroyer
Year: 2006   **Set Number:** 6211
Pieces: 1,367   **Films:** IV, V, & VI
Dimensions:
length 74.4 cm (29 in)
width 38.4 cm (15 in)
height 9.3 cm (3.7 in)
Minifigures: 8 (Darth Vader, Grand Moff Tarkin, Imperial officer, two stormtroopers and two Imperial guards, R2-Q5)

Cloud City

After the Battle of Hoth, Han Solo and Chewbacca escape with Leia and C-3PO to a floating pleasure resort and mining colony called Cloud City, located near a gas planet called Bespin. Its administrator, Lando Calrissian, is Han Solo's longtime friend and sometime rival. The arrival of Solo and the others, however, is preceeded by Boba Fett and Darth Vader, who spring a trap and lure Luke Skywalker to a confrontation with Vader himself!

LEIA (BESPIN OUTFIT)

LEIA ORGANA
In the luxurious surroundings of Cloud City, Leia changes clothes, lets down her hair and ties it back. Succumbing to Solo's charms, she has only a brief time to relax before she is ensnared in Vader's trap.

▽ Duel with Vader

When Luke arrives at Cloud City to rescue his friends, Vader is waiting for him in the carbon freezing chamber. They ignite their lightsabres and duel through the chamber into a control room overlooking a huge reactor shaft. Luke is sucked through a smashed window and their final clash takes place on a treacherous gantry.

Viewport

Pipes in control room

Mechanism allows wall to drop

Sculpture

Doorway to landing platform

Balcony over reactor shaft

Mechanism to open viewport

Dining room table

COLLAPSING WALLS
Darth Vader uses the Force to throw objects at Luke. Watch out for that collapsing wall, Luke!

THROUGH THE WINDOW
A viewport breaks open and a vacuum sucks Luke onto a narrow maintenance gantry, where the final confrontation occurs.

▽ Landing Platform

Arriving starships usually dock on a landing platform outside the main wall of Cloud City. When Han and the others arrive in the *Millennium Falcon*, Lando Calrissian meets him. Later, he escorts Han and his friends to a dining room – but it's a trap. The Dark Lord of the Sith and his stormtroopers are waiting to capture them.

BESPIN GUARD
Sergeant Edian is a loyal member of the Bespin security forces, called the Wing Guard. He helps escort the carbon-frozen Han Solo onto Boba Fett's Slave I and his minifigure appears in set 6209.

SERGEANT EDIAN

Landing lights

Entrance walkway

Carbon Freezing Chamber

HAN SOLO IN CARBONITE

Vader intends to carbon freeze Luke for transport to the Emperor, and decides to test the process on Han Solo. Watched by Calrissian, Vader and Fett, Solo is lowered into the freezing chamber: He emerges frozen into a block of carbonite.

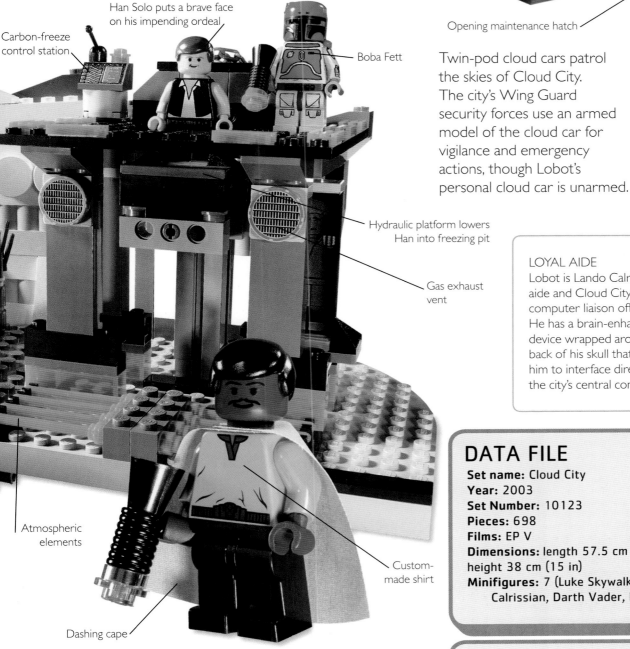

Han Solo puts a brave face on his impending ordeal

Carbon-freeze control station

Boba Fett

Hydraulic platform lowers Han into freezing pit

Gas exhaust vent

Atmospheric elements

Custom-made shirt

Dashing cape

LANDO CALRISSIAN

Lando Calrissian is an ex-cardshark who used his winning charms and sartorial style to become the baron-administrator of Cloud City. At first, Vader forces him to betray Solo, but Lando turns against the Imperials and eventually becomes a general in the Rebel Alliance.

Cloud Car

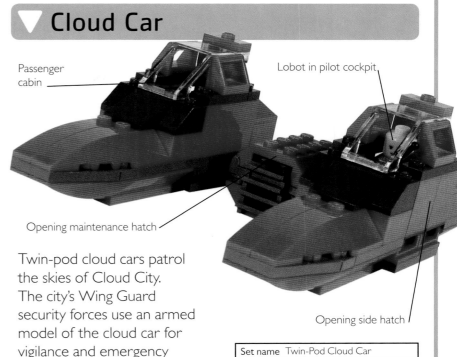

Passenger cabin

Lobot in pilot cockpit

Opening maintenance hatch

Opening side hatch

Twin-pod cloud cars patrol the skies of Cloud City. The city's Wing Guard security forces use an armed model of the cloud car for vigilance and emergency actions, though Lobot's personal cloud car is unarmed.

Set name	Twin-Pod Cloud Car	
Year 2002	Number 7119	
Pieces 117	Film EP V	

LOYAL AIDE
Lobot is Lando Calrissian's aide and Cloud City's computer liaison officer. He has a brain-enhancing device wrapped around the back of his skull that enables him to interface directly with the city's central computer.

LOBOT

DATA FILE

Set name: Cloud City
Year: 2003
Set Number: 10123
Pieces: 698
Films: EP V
Dimensions: length 57.5 cm (22.6 in); width 7 cm (2.8 in); height 38 cm (15 in)
Minifigures: 7 (Luke Skywalker, Han Solo, Leia Organa, Lando Calrissian, Darth Vader, Boba Fett and stormtrooper)

BRICK FACTS

● Boba Fett with printed arms and legs and Lando Calrissian in his usual outfit are exclusive to this set. (In Jabba's Sail Barge, set 6210, Lando is in disguise.)

Rebel Alliance

Freedom fighters who have banded together as the Rebel Alliance are dedicated to the Empire's downfall. Some Rebels are deserters from the Imperial forces, but many are untrained volunteers. With skilful leaders and a ragtag assortment of ships and weapons, the Rebels prove a serious threat to Emperor Palpatine's iron rule.

▼ Y-Wing

BTL-A4 Y-wings are the most numerous fighters in the Rebel fleet, famously employed in the attack on the first Death Star (the set comes with a TIE fighter). They have hyperdrives, ion fission engines and massive firepower, including ion cannons and laser cannons.

Set name	TIE Fighter & Y-Wing	
Year 2002	Number	7152
Pieces 407	Film	EP IV & VI

Extended engine nacelles

Sensor dome

Swivelling twin ion cannons

Laser tip

REBEL MECHANIC

Rebel engineers and technicians maintain and repair spaceships and vehicles, among other tasks.

▼ Rebel Scout Speeder

The Rebels use these military-grade repulsorlift speeders for patrol and reconnaissance. They seat a pilot, gunner and two soldiers. The rotating heavy laser cannon detaches for use as a static emplacement.

Blast helmet with visor and extended neck guard

Laser cannon firing tip

Set name	Rebel Scout Speeder	
Year 2008	Number	7668
Pieces 82	Film	EU

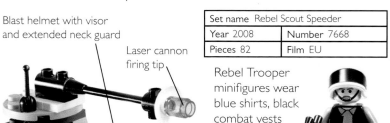

Rebel Trooper minifigures wear blue shirts, black combat vests and grey trousers.

REBEL TROOPER

A280 blaster rifle

DH-17 blaster

Rebel insignia

Astromech co-pilot in droid socket

Thrust vectral ring

Set name	Y-Wing Fighter	
Year 2007	Number	7658
Pieces 454	Film	EP IV & VI

Deflector shield generator

Ion jet engine

Cockpit controls

Custom helmet

Rebel unit marking

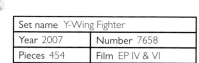

BRICK FACTS

● Leia Organa's minifigure in her white Alderaan gown has a yellow face in *Millennium Falcon* (set 7190) and a flesh-coloured face in Death Star (set 10188) and *Millennium Falcon* (set 10179).

● *Home One* Mon Calamari Star Cruiser (set 7754) won the 2009 Fan's Choice Set (runners up were The Arrest of Palpatine and *Slave II*/Cloud City Landing Platform).

DAK RALTER

Luke's snowspeeder gunner appears in both Snowspeeder sets (4500 and 7130) and Hoth Rebel Base (set 7666).

BIGGS DARKLIGHTER

Biggs Darklighter is killed on the attack on the first Death Star. His minifigure comes with X-wing Fighter (set 7140).

DUTCH VANDER

Y-wing pilot Dutch Vander's face is yellow in TIE Fighter & Y-wing (set 7150) and flesh-coloured in Y-Wing Fighter (set 7658).

Tantive IV

As a Senator for Alderaan, Princess Leia Organa travels in a diplomatic starship, the *Tantive IV*. The ship also carries out covert missions for the Rebel Alliance, until Darth Vader pursues the ship and captures it.

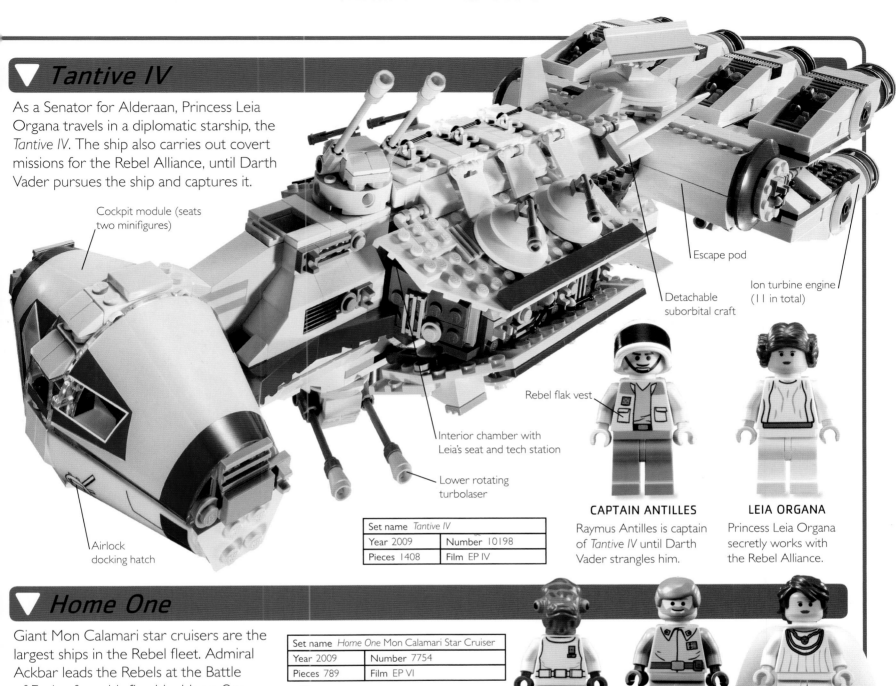

Cockpit module (seats two minifigures)

Escape pod

Ion turbine engine (11 in total)

Detachable suborbital craft

Rebel flak vest

Interior chamber with Leia's seat and tech station

Lower rotating turbolaser

Airlock docking hatch

Set name	*Tantive IV*	
Year 2009	Number 10198	
Pieces 1408	Film EP IV	

CAPTAIN ANTILLES
Raymus Antilles is captain of *Tantive IV* until Darth Vader strangles him.

LEIA ORGANA
Princess Leia Organa secretly works with the Rebel Alliance.

Home One

Giant Mon Calamari star cruisers are the largest ships in the Rebel fleet. Admiral Ackbar leads the Rebels at the Battle of Endor from his flagship, *Home One*. The set contains the bridge, command centre and hangar for an A-wing.

Set name	*Home One* Mon Calamari Star Cruiser	
Year 2009	Number 7754	
Pieces 789	Film EP VI	

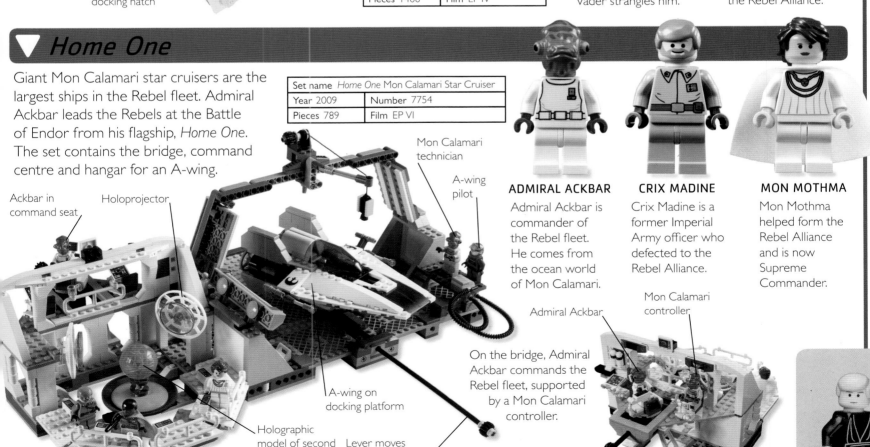

Ackbar in command seat

Holoprojector

Mon Calamari technician

A-wing pilot

A-wing on docking platform

Holographic model of second Death Star

Lever moves docking platform

ADMIRAL ACKBAR
Admiral Ackbar is commander of the Rebel fleet. He comes from the ocean world of Mon Calamari.

CRIX MADINE
Crix Madine is a former Imperial Army officer who defected to the Rebel Alliance.

MON MOTHMA
Mon Mothma helped form the Rebel Alliance and is now Supreme Commander.

Admiral Ackbar

Mon Calamari controller

On the bridge, Admiral Ackbar commands the Rebel fleet, supported by a Mon Calamari controller.

BRIDGE

Echo Base

On the ice planet Hoth, the Rebel Alliance establishes its secret Echo Base, protected by an immense energy shield. When the Empire discovers the location of the base, it deploys AT-ATs and AT-STs to destroy the shield generator. The combined strength of Rebel artillery emplacements and snowspeeder squadrons cannot prevent one of the worst battlefield defeats for the Alliance.

Imperial Probe Droid

Probe droids (or probots) are programmed to seek out the Rebels and report back to Imperial officers. A probot detects telltale signs of habitation on Hoth, prompting Vader to initiate a full-scale Imperial assault.

Photoreceptor

Sensor limb

Set name	Hoth Rebel Base	
Year	2007	Number 7666
Pieces	548	Film EP V

Hoth Base

Huge blast doors and DF9 anti-infantry battery protect the north entrance of the Rebel base. Inside the doors, the Rebels have constructed a large hangar for X-wings and snowspeeders, which are serviced by a variety of repair and maintenance racks.

Monitoring console screen

Tool rack

Cogs open and close doors

Ice-cut pillar

Guide light

Blast door

Control panel

Ice mountain

Rotating snowspeeder docking clamp

NORTH ENTRANCE (EXTERIOR VIEW)

Repulsorlifts

Snowspeeder engine

MAINTENANCE CRANE
Rebel pilots and technicians use cranes to unload supplies and remove vehicle engines for repair.

Set name	Hoth Rebel Base	
Year	2007	Number 7666
Pieces	548	Film EP V

K-3PO
K-3PO is a white protocol droid who was given the rank of lieutenant in the Rebel Alliance.

Turret Defense

Gunner's hatch

In trenches and behind snow-packed ridges, supported by tall, cylindrical anti-infantry batteries, Rebel soldiers are the first line of defence against Imperial walkers.

Laser barrel

Power conduit

Rebel soldier

Targeting crew hatch

Snow wall

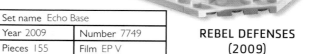

Set name	Echo Base	
Year	2009	Number 7749
Pieces	155	Film EP V

REBEL DEFENSES (2009)

DF.9 BATTERY (2007)

Set name	Hoth Rebel Base	
Year	2007	Number 7666
Pieces	548	Film EP V

Rebel Soldier

Rebel soldiers on Hoth wear insulated uniforms and backpacks. They have yellow faces, red fringes and helmet visors in the 1999 Snowspeeder (set 7130); they have the same faces but with snow goggles in the 2004 Snowspeeder (set 4500). Their faces are flesh-coloured in the 2007 Hoth Rebel Base (set 7666). Troops wear new-style goggles in the 2009 Echo Base (set 7749).

REBEL SOLDIER (1999)

REBEL SOLDIER (2004)

REBEL SOLDIER (2007)

REBEL SOLDIER (2009)

Snowspeeder

Rebel snowspeeders are civilian T-47 airspeeders adapted for military use with laser cannons bolted to the wings, as well as souped-up engines and armour plating (but no shields).

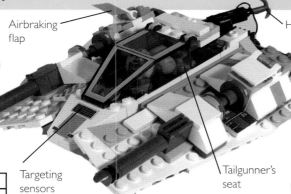

Airbraking flap

Harpoon gun

Targeting sensors

Tailgunner's seat

SNOWSPEEDER (2004)

The 1999 and 2004 models both have seats for Luke and Dak Ralter; the 2004 model also has a harpoon tow cable.

SNOWSPEEDER (1999)

Set name	Snowspeeder	
Year	1999	Number 7130
Pieces	212	Film EP V

Set name	Rebel Snowspeeder	
Year	2004	Number 4500
Pieces	214	Film EP V

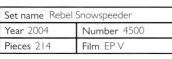

TOW CABLE
Luke Skywalker cleverly circles his tow cable around all four of the AT-AT's legs, causing the walker to topple over.

Power convertor

Laser cannon

Harpoon and tow cable

Repulsor unit housing

The 2007 snowspeeder seats Luke and Dak, with space in the cockpit for Luke's lightsabre. The harpoon is ready for firing at an AT-AT's leg and the engines are removable for repair.

SNOWSPEEDER (2007)

Set name	Hoth Rebel Base	
Year	2007	Number 7666
Pieces	548	Film EP V

Tauntaun

Rebel troops on Hoth make patrols on domesticated snow lizards called tauntauns, which can withstand freezing winds but are not the sweetest smelling of animals.

Horn

Saddle

Han Solo

Claws

Set name	Echo Base	
Year	2009	Number 7749
Pieces	155	Film EP V

BRICK FACTS

- The 1999 and 2004 Snowspeeder sets include a dish-shaped anti-vehicle artillery P-Tower, used against AT-ATs, flying vehicles and snowtroopers.

Main Entrance

C-3PO and R2-D2 tremble at the entry portcullis to Jabba's Palace (at least, C-3PO does!). A gatewatcher droid pokes its single photoreceptor from a slot in the door and passes news of their arrival to Jabba's henchman, Bib Fortuna, who interrogates them.

Set name	Jabba's Message	
Year 2003	Number 4475	
Pieces 44	Film EP VI	

Door slides open

Gatewatcher droid

R2-D2

C-3PO

Jabba's Palace

Jabba the Hutt runs an extensive crime empire from his fortress-palace on Tatooine. The entire complex is overrun with gangsters, bounty hunters, exotic creatures, corrupt droids, entertainers and servants. This den of vice is also where Han Solo encased in carbonite is displayed – and from where Han's friends must rescue him.

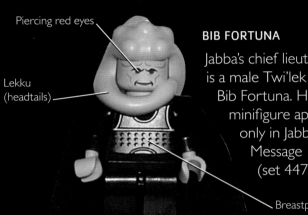

Piercing red eyes

BIB FORTUNA
Jabba's chief lieutenant is a male Twi'lek called Bib Fortuna. His minifigure appears only in Jabba's Message (set 4475).

Lekku (headtails)

Dim lights

Breastplate

B'OMARR MONK
Jabba shares his palace with the original owners: B'omarr monks. These monks dispense with their bodies when they reach enlightenment, leaving only their brains in nutrient jars. Automated legs carry the brain jars throughout the palace.

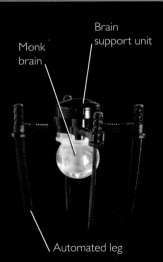

Monk brain

Brain support unit

Automated leg

Throne Room

Jabba the Hutt sits atop a dais in his dimly lit throne room, within reach of a bowl of his favourite snack, slimy gorgs. He controls everything in the room, including a trap-door that leads to a pit below. Enslaved Princess Leia has no choice but to watch as Jabba deals harshly with Luke Skywalker, now wearing the robes of a Jedi Knight. Beneath the throne room, droid supervisor EV-9D9 shows no mercy to a lost GNK droid.

Power coupler outlet

Jabba's sadistic supervisor of cyborg operations, EV-9D9, enjoys watching other droids suffer.

EV-9D9

BRICK FACTS

- Jabba's Message (set 4475) and Jabba's Prize (set 4476) can clip onto the sides of Jabba's Palace (set 4480).

- Leia as Jabba's slave has a yellow face with Jabba's Palace and a flesh-coloured face with Jabba's Sail Barge (set 6210).

Trophy Wall

In one of the recesses of the throne room, Jabba displays his prized trophy: Han Solo flash-frozen in carbonite.

Set name	Jabba's Prize	
Year 2003	Number 4476	
Pieces 39	Film EP VI	

Jabba is a gigantic slug-like Hutt, with slimy skin, an unfathomable appetite and a large, lascivious mouth.

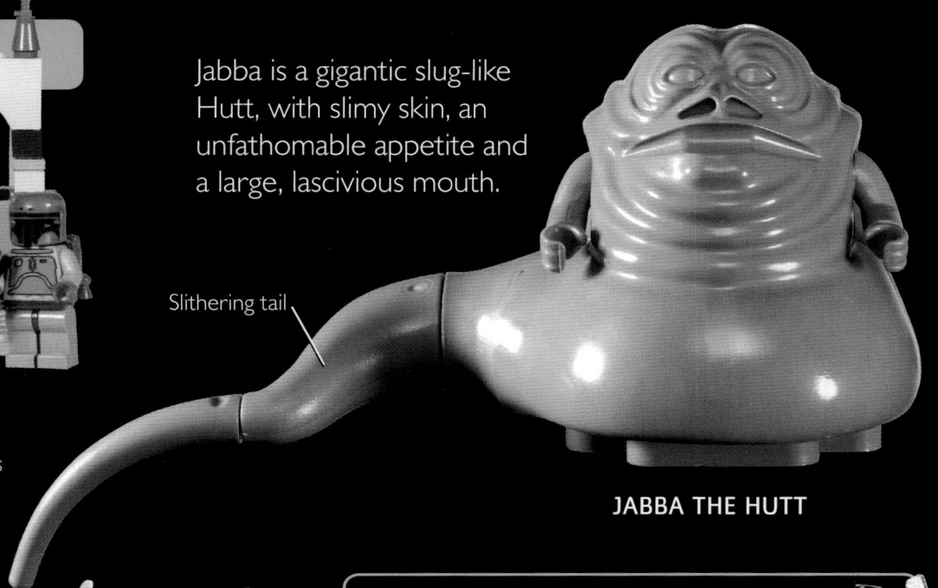

Slithering tail

JABBA THE HUTT

Throne moves back to open trap-door

Neck brace and chain

GAMORREAN GUARD
Dim-witted, brutish Gamorreans act as Jabba's bodyguards. They wield vibro-axe weapons rather than blasters. In Jabba's Prize (set 4476), their arms are grey; in Jabba's Sail Barge (set 6210), their arms are brown.

Vibro-axe

Jabba the Hutt seated on dais

Gorg bowl

Set name	Jabba's Palace	
Year 2003	Number 4480	
Pieces 234	Film EP VI	

B'omarr monk

Trap-door

Droid 'assessment' room

EV-9D9

GNK droid

65

Jabba's Sail Barge

Jabba's Sail Barge is a giant repulsorlift pleasure craft that carries the crime lord and his undesirable entourage from his palace to Podraces, gladiatorial contests and other shadier activities. It also transports Jabba to the Great Pit of Carkoon to watch Luke Skywalker being fed to the hungry beast that inhabits this basin in the desert.

Decorative sails for shade, rather than propulsion

Forward deck catapult

Cockpit (beneath hull plating)

DESERT SKIFF
The 2000 version of the sand skiff comes with minifigures of Luke (with a lightsabre) and Han (with a spear).

Set name	Desert Skiff	
Year	2000	Number 7104
Pieces	53	Film EP VI

Narrow plank

Sand Skiff

Gamorrean guard

Prison cell

Kitchen

Sarlacc Pit

Beaked tongue

Steering vane

Teeth prevent victims from escaping

R2-D2
Poor R2! Jabba has forced on him the indignity of serving drinks to his guests.

Sand skiffs are repulsorlift platforms used to ferry passengers or prisoners to and from Jabba's palace. Luke is forced to walk the extensible plank over the Sarlacc pit.

Deck gun (added by Jabba for protection from rival gangs)

Jabba prepares to watch his victims' last moments

Aft deck

R2-D2 (with drinks tray)

DATA FILE

Set name: Jabba's Sail Barge
Year: 2006
Set Number: 6210
Pieces: 781
Film: EP VI
Dimensions: Sail Barge: length 46 cm (18 in); Sand Skiff: length 20 cm (8 in)
Minifigures: 8 (Jabba the Hutt, Luke Skywalker, Han Solo, Princess Leia, Lando Calrissian, R2-D2, Boba Fett and Gamorrean guard)

Hinged shutters

Gorg snack bowl

Thrust exhaust

For years, Jabba has enjoyed feeding his enemies to the Sarlacc at Carkoon. All that can be seen of the Sarlacc is its beaked tongue. The rest of its huge, tentacled body is hidden below the surface.

Hinged boarding hatch to observation lounge

Face guard

UNDERCOVER AGENT
Who's this mean-looking skiff guard? Don't tell Jabba, but it's Lando Calrissian in disguise. Dresssed as a lowly guard, he gains access to Jabba's Palace and helps rescue Han at the Sarlacc pit.

Bounty hunter Boba Fett can be launched into the air using a deck-mounted catapult, just as if he were powered by his jetpack!

▼ A-Wing

The Rebels constructed this small, lightning-fast ship in secrecy before the Battle of Endor as an escort craft. A trio of A-wing starfighters play a crucial role in the battle, destroying Darth Vader's gigantic ship, the *Executor*.

Reinforced front section can ram enemy ships

2000

A-WING PILOT

Set name	A-Wing Fighter	
Year 2000	Number 7134	
Pieces 123	Film EP VI	

Transparisteel cockpit canopy

Swivel-mounted laser cannon

Maintenance diagnostic system

Cargo hold

2006

Set name	A-Wing Fighter	
Year 2006	Number 6207	
Pieces 194	Film EP VI	

The 2006 A-wing comes with a pilot, technician and cargo sled. The ship's cockpit viewscreen shows a Star Destroyer in range!

Fusion reactor exhaust

Repulsorlift cargo sled

▶ B-Wing (2000)

Rebel-designed B-wing starfighters are attack vessels that target the Empire's capital ships. They are well-armed with heavy laser cannons, ion cannons, and proton torpedo launchers.

REBEL COMMAND CENTER

Secondary proton torpedo launcher

Ion cannon

Retro thrust nozzles

Repulsorlift crane/tools sled

Set name	B-Wing at Rebel Command Center	
Year 2000	Number 7180	
Pieces 338	Film EP VI	

The Rebels command their forces at Endor from a mobile command centre on board a massive Mon Calamari star cruiser. A-wings, B-wings, X-wings, and Y-wings are launched from hangars in the ship as well.

Battle of Endor

The Battle of Endor takes place on the surface of Endor's forest moon and in orbit around the planet. The Empire's second Death Star orbits the moon, protected by a defensive shield projected from a generator on the moon's surface. The Rebels must concentrate all their resources on a concerted strike that will ultimately bring down the hated Empire.

▶ B-Wing (2006)

This B-wing model docks vertically at a service/refueling tower (regular B-wings land on their side with folded wings). The ship can deploy its S-foil wings for flight and its weapons are operated by flick-firing mechanisms.

Set name	B-Wing Fighter	
Year 2006	Number 6208	
Pieces 435	Film EP VI	

Hinged cockpit canopy

Engine thrust nozzle

Main heat radiator

Energy cell for anti-gravity generator

Main wing

B-wing pilot Ten Numb

Maintenance platform

Targeting laser

Heavy laser cannon

▼ Ewok Weapons

Endor's forest moon is inhabited by Ewoks, who help the Rebels defeat the Imperial forces guarding the shield generator bunker (including, with this set, a stormtrooper and a scout trooper on a speeder bike). The Ewoks use weapons that are crude — simple wooden catapults and gliders — but these furry creatures are tough and resourceful.

Light framework

GLIDER (2002)

Wicket (brown hood)

Animal pelt wing

CATAPULT (2002)

Push down to fire!

Tension wheel

Set name	Ewok Attack	
Year 2002	Number 7139	
Pieces 119	Film EP VI	

GLIDER (2009)

CATAPULT (2009)

Ewok spear

Hunting trophies

Animal pelt hood

Set name	The Battle of Endor	
Year 2009	Number 8038	
Pieces 887	Film EP IV	

Spare rocks

Plants for camouflage

Ewok scout's hood

Orange hood

PAPLOO

WICKET W WARRICK

CHIEF CHIRPA

S-foil wing in deployed position

▼ Shield Generator Bunker

The Imperial shield generator is operated from a bunker on Endor's moon. A Rebel commando team, led by Han Solo, Princess Leia and Chewbacca (and two commandos), must evade two Imperial scout troopers to gain entry to the secret back entrance and overpower the Death Star trooper inside.

Sliding blast doors (can be 'blown off')

FRONT

Set name	The Battle of Endor	
Year 2009	Number 8038	
Pieces 887	Film EP IV	

Control monitor

Blaster rack

Red-suited B-wing pilot

Forest vegetation

Power generator array

Death Star trooper

Jedi Command

During the Clone Wars, the Jedi must forego their traditional role as peacemakers and take on military roles. Many become generals in the republic army, fighting alongside clone commanders and clone troops on numerous battlefronts.

The *Twilight*

Anakin's personal starship in the Clone Wars is a battered Corellian G9 Rigger freighter, the *Twilight*. Anakin first 'borrows' the damaged ship from a landing platform on Teth, when he and Ahsoka are rescuing Jabba the Hutt's son, Rotta. Anakin has since repaired and upgraded its weapons and systems.

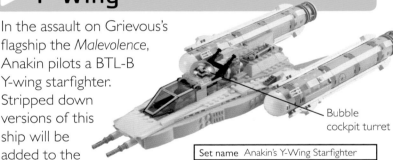

Laser turret

Wingtip blaster

Deployable escape pod

Interior hold includes working two-cable winch

Set name	The *Twilight*	
Year 2008	Number	7680
Pieces 882	Film	CW

ROTTA

In one mission, Anakin and Ahsoka have to rescue Jabba the Hutt's squishy son, Rotta.

Y-Wing

In the assault on Grievous's flagship the *Malevolence*, Anakin pilots a BTL-B Y-wing starfighter. Stripped down versions of this ship will be added to the Rebel fleet.

Bubble cockpit turret

Set name	Anakin's Y-Wing Starfighter	
Year 2009	Number	8037
Pieces 570	Film	CW

▼ Jedi Starfighters

During the Clone Wars, many Jedi pilot single-seater Delta-7B *Aethersprite* starfighters, with astromech copilots. The ship features flick-firing missiles, retractable landing gear and an ejection button for the astromechs.

Set name	Ahsoka's Starfighter and Vulture Droid	
Year 2009	Number	7751
Pieces 291	Film	CW

Enemy buzz droid

R7-A7

AHSOKA'S STARFIGHTER

Set name	Anakin's Jedi Starfighter	
Year 2008	Number	7669
Pieces 153	Film	CW

R2-D2

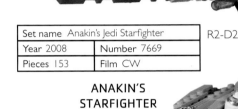

ANAKIN'S STARFIGHTER

Laser cannon

R7-A7
Ahsoka's prototype R7 unit acts as copilot on missions.

Growing head-tails

Scar from encounter with Asajj Ventress

Black surcoat

ANAKIN SKYWALKER

In the Clone Wars, Anakin is a hot-headed Jedi Knight with unkempt hair and a long scar on his face.

Montrals (hollow head growths)

AHSOKA TANO

Young Ahsoka Tano is Anakin Skywalker's Jedi Padawan. She is a Togruta, a species with colourful skin and two long 'head-tails'.

Armour plates

OBI-WAN KENOBI

General Obi-Wan Kenobi wears black gloves and clone-trooper armour plating over his Jedi robes.

Green lightsabre blade

Sensitive ears

YODA

Grand Master Yoda wears a simple robe and brown tunic. He comes with Armored Assault Tank (set 8018).

Purple lightsabre blade

MACE WINDU

Jedi Master Mace Windu appears in Republic Attack Shuttle (set 8019) with a tan robe and steely expression.

Protective goggles and breath mask

PLO KOON

Jedi Master Plo Koon wears an anti-oxygen mask and comes with Republic Gunship (set 7676).

Separatist Command

Count Dooku leads the Separatists, but secretly takes orders from Darth Sidious. He commands droid fleets and armies sponsored by member worlds and trade groups, chief among them the Trade Federation, led by Nute Gunray.

MagnaGuard Starfighter

Grievous's MagnaGuards fly modified P-38 starfighters, built on Utapau, where Grievous established a secret headquarters. P-38s attack Anakin and Ahsoka as they escape from Teth in the *Twilight*.

Set name	MagnaGuard Starfighter	
Year 2008	Number 7673	
Pieces 431	Film CW	

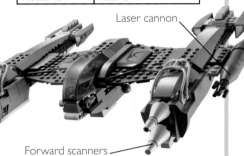

Laser cannon

Forward scanners

Solar Sailer

Count Dooku's personal starship is an elegant Geonosian Solar Sailer. Piloted by an FA-4 droid, Dooku and two MagnaGuards travel to battlefields, where Dooku uses his speeder bike to meet Separatist leaders.

Opening rear hatch

Cockpit sphere

Set name	Count Dooku's Solar Sailer	
Year 2009	Number 7752	
Pieces 385	Film CW	

Power receptor nodule

Wings split in flight

Separatist Shuttle

Nute Gunray travels in a *Sheathipede*-class shuttle flown by a battle droid pilot, with two battle droids for security (Neimoidians are cowardly).

Set name	Separatist Shuttle	
Year 2009	Number 8036	
Pieces 259	Film CW	

Cockpit hood

Assassin Droid

IG-series assassin droids are mercenaries programmed for stealth and destruction. They sometimes utilise speeder bikes on missions.

Steering vane

Blaster rifle

Regular (silver) assassin droid

Set name	Assassin Droids Battle Pack	
Year 2009	Number 8015	
Pieces 94	Film CW	

ELITE (BLACK) ASSASSIN DROID

Neimoidian headdress

Claw legs unfold for landing

Wings project deflector shield

Curved lightsabre hilt

Facial tattoos

Electrostaff

Hologram of Death Star plans

COUNT DOOKU

The public leader of the Separatists is Count Dooku, also known as the Sith Lord Darth Tyranus.

ASAJJ VENTRESS

Asajj Ventress trained as a Jedi but turned to the dark side. She fights using two paired curved-hilt lightsabres.

MAGNAGUARD

Grievous's elite droid bodyguards carry electrostaff weapons and often fight in pairs.

NUTE GUNRAY

The leader of the wealthy Trade Federation is a Neimoidian called Nute Gunray.

ONACONDA FARR

The Senator for Rodia turns to the Trade Federation for help for his starving planet.

PALPATINE

Supreme Chancellor Palpatine is leader of the Republic, but secretly he's plotting its downfall.

V-19 Torrent Starfighter

This fast, agile assault fighter features wing-mounted laser cannons and concussion missile launchers. The wings extend in flight and close for landing, allowing the clone pilot access to the cockpit via a sliding hatch.

Concussion missile launcher

Powerful thruster

Ventral airfoil

Set name V-19 Torrent	
Year 2008	Number 7674
Pieces 471	Film CW

Clone Army

The Republic Army is made up of a large fleet of ships, a range of land vehicles, and millions of clone soldiers. Troopers are led by clone commanders who report to Jedi Generals, who lead the fight against the Separatist threat.

AT-TE Walker

AT-TE walkers carry clone troopers into battle. The set features Anakin Skywalker, Ahsoka Tano, Captain Rex, a clone trooper and Rotta. A battle droid on a blue STAP is also included.

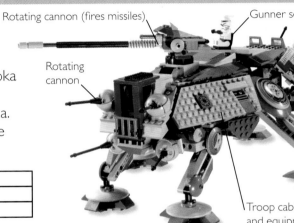

Rotating cannon (fires missiles)

Gunner seat

Rotating cannon

Articulated leg

Troop cabin with seats and equipment

Set name AT-TE Walker	
Year 2008	Number 7675
Pieces 798	Film CW

Captain Rex

Clone captain Rex is Anakin's second-in-command. His minifigure wears a kama and pauldron, and carries two commando pistols. Under his helmet is his clone face.

Jaig eyes (battle honours)

Kama (flexible anti-blast armour)

Republic Attack Shuttle

The *Nu*-class attack shuttle is a fast, long-range gunship, with heavy armour, powerful shields and a range of laser weaponry, though this model is also equipped to drop missiles from a bomb hatch on the underside. A clone pilot flies the ship, which carries Mace Windu and a clone trooper into battle.

Clone pilot

Laser cannon

Set name Republic Attack Shuttle	
Year 2009	Number 8019
Pieces 636	Film CW

Fold-down wings

Dropship

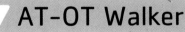

Low Altitide Assault Transport/carriers (LAAT/c, or dropships) carry tanks (AT-OTs and AT-TEs) into battlezones. The ship blasts flick-firing missiles from its rotating laser cannons.

Magnets hold walker

Nose art (choice of stickers)

Set name Republic Dropship with AT-OT	
Year 2009	Number 10195
Pieces 1,758	Film CW

AT-OT Walker

Set name Republic Dropship with AT-OT	
Year 2009	Number 10195
Pieces 1,758	Film CW

Open-topped All Terrain Open Transports (AT-OTs) are not designed to be tanks, but to transport troops and cargo in safe zones.

16 troop positions

Cabin splits open

Commander Cody

Cody is a clone commander assigned to General Kenobi. His minifigure carries two commando pistols and wears ARC armor.

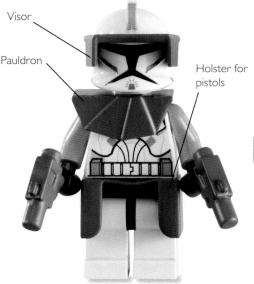

Visor

Pauldron

Holster for pistols

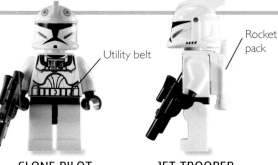

Utility belt

Rocket pack

CLONE PILOT

Pilots in the Clone Wars have yellow markings and red Republic symbols on their helmets.

JET TROOPER

Jet troopers carry out aerial missions. Two come with Corporate Alliance Tank Droid (set 7748).

CLONE TROOPER

In the Clone Wars, clone troopers wear Phase I white armor and carry blasters.

SENATE COMMANDO

Commandos are specially trained non-clones who protect Senators on Coruscant.

Republic Attack Gunship

Clone soldiers depend on gunships to ferry them into and out of battlefields. This one can be customized either as Crumb Bomber (with Kowakian monkey lizard) or Lucky Lekku (with female Twi'lek).

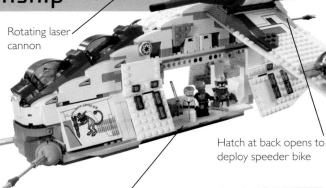

Rotating laser cannon

Hatch at back opens to deploy speeder bike

Opening troop bay door

Set name Republic Attack Gunship	
Year 2008	Number 7676
Pieces 1,034	Film CW

Republic Fighter Tank

Set name Republic Fighter Tank	
Year 2008	Number 7679
Pieces 592	Film CW

The TX-130 *Saber*-class fighter vehicle is a fast-attack tank equipped with laser cannons and concussion missiles. Clone troopers pilot this tank, though many Jedi also drive them during the Clone Wars.

Flick-fire laser cannon

Sensor antenna

Gunner in elevating seat

"Hovers" on hidden wheels

Clone soldier on patrol

Clone Walker

The two-person walker comes with two clone troopers, a clone gunner, a clone commander, and ARC trooper gear.

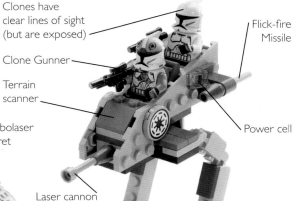

Clones have clear lines of sight (but are exposed)

Clone Gunner

Terrain scanner

Flick-fire Missile

Power cell

Laser cannon

Set name Clone Walker Battle Pack	
Year 2009	Number 8014
Pieces 72	Film CW

Venator-Class Republic Attack Cruiser

The precursor to the Imperial Star Destroyer, the *Venator*-class attack cruiser has enough firepower to blast through Separatist battleships with ease. The interior hangar carries Supreme Chancellor Palpatine and two Senate commandos, while the crew comprises a clone pilot and a clone gunner.

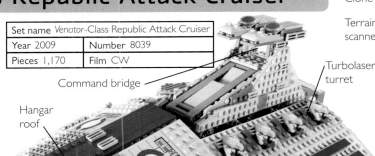

Set name *Venator*-Class Republic Attack Cruiser	
Year 2009	Number 8039
Pieces 1,170	Film CW

Command bridge

Turbolaser turret

Hangar roof

Open Circle armada's emblem

Dual turbolaser

Droid Army

Under the command of Count Dooku, the wealthy Separatist war machine is able to amass a terrifying range of specialist droids and attack vehicles. As the Clone Wars progress, new battlefronts are opened on diverse worlds across the galaxy.

▼ Armoured Assault Tank

This repulsorlift AAT floats into battle armed with laser weapons and carrying two battle droids and three super battle droids (who face off against Yoda and a clone trooper). A speeder bike can be deployed from the rear for high-speed strike/reconnaissance missions.

Set name	AAT	
Year 2009	Number 8018	
Pieces 407	Film CW	

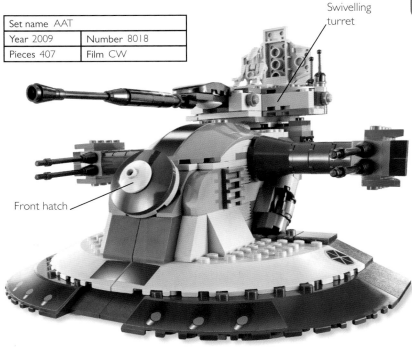

Swivelling turret

Front hatch

▶ Dwarf Spider Droid

Set name	Hailfire Droid and Spider Droid	
Year 2008	Number 7670	
Pieces 249	Film CW	

Dwarf spider droids are mobile laser cannon turrets that walk into battle in advance of battle droids.

Tracing antenna

Laser cannon

▶ Vulture Fighter

No Jedi likes to see a swarm of deadly Vulture droids heading their way. This model carries a payload of two buzz droids.

Set name	Ahsoka's Starfighter & Vulture Droid	
Year 2009	Number 7751	
Pieces 291	Film CW	

Sensor eyes (printed)

Wings convert to legs

Flick-launching missile

▼ Tank Droid

Amphibious NR-N99 tank droids roll into battle on high-traction caterpillar treads. In the Clone Wars, they were deployed in battles on many worlds, including Geonosis, Kashyyyk and Cato Neimoidia. Deployed side by side, they form an unstoppable wall of armour, obliterating everything in its path.

Photoreceptor eye

Pontoon tread

Set name	Corporate Alliance Tank Droid	
Year 2009	Number 7748	
Pieces 216	Film CW	

▶ Spider Droid

Homing spider droids can cover great distances on their all-terrain legs. Their sensors lock onto enemy targets and their dish-shaped laser cannons provide sustained fire.

Stilt leg

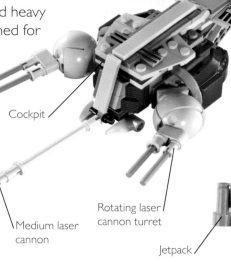

▶ Droid Gunship

Droid gunships are well-shielded heavy missile platforms (HMPs) designed for sub-orbital air strikes. They are relatively slow to manoeuvre but their firepower is devastating. Droid brains usually control the gunships but this modified version includes a cockpit for a battle droid pilot.

Cog turns to drop missiles

Rangefinder

Cockpit

Dedicated blaster arm

Rotating laser cannon turret

Medium laser cannon

Jetpack

SUPER BATTLE DROID

The B2 super battle droid is equipped with a dedicated blaster arm.

Set name	Droid Gunship	
Year	2008	Number 7678
Pieces	329	Film CW

ROCKET BATTLE DROID

These orange-coloured battle droids are equipped with jetpacks for space combat. They come with the Hyena droid bomber (set 8016).

BATTLE DROID COMMANDER

Clone Wars-era battle droid commanders feature yellow markings on the chest only (earlier models had yellow heads as well).

PIRATE TANK

Led by Honda Ohnaka, Weequay pirates on the planet Florrum use spaceships, speeder bikes and tanks.

Set name	Pirate Tank	
Year	2009	Number 7753
Pieces	372	Film CW

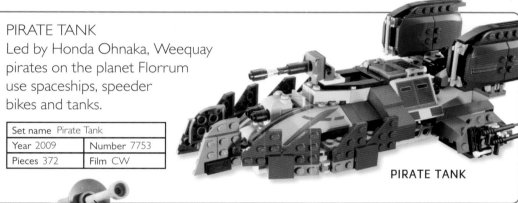

PIRATE TANK

Moveable surface-to-air missile

▼ Hyena Droid Bomber

Hyena-class droid bombers are modified vulture fighters, with a secondary cockpit sensor 'head' for improved target scoping and upgraded weapons systems, including concussion missile launchers. Notoriously, Hyena droid bombers perform carpet-bombing raids on Twi'lek cities during the Battle of Ryloth.

Set name	Hyena Droid Bomber	
Year	2009	Number 8016
Pieces	232	Film CW

Reactor sphere and droid brain

Droid brain unit

Concussion missiles drop from underneath

Swivelling surface-to-surface laser cannons

Laser cannons

Set name	Separatist Spider Droid	
Year	2008	Number 7681
Pieces	206	Film CW

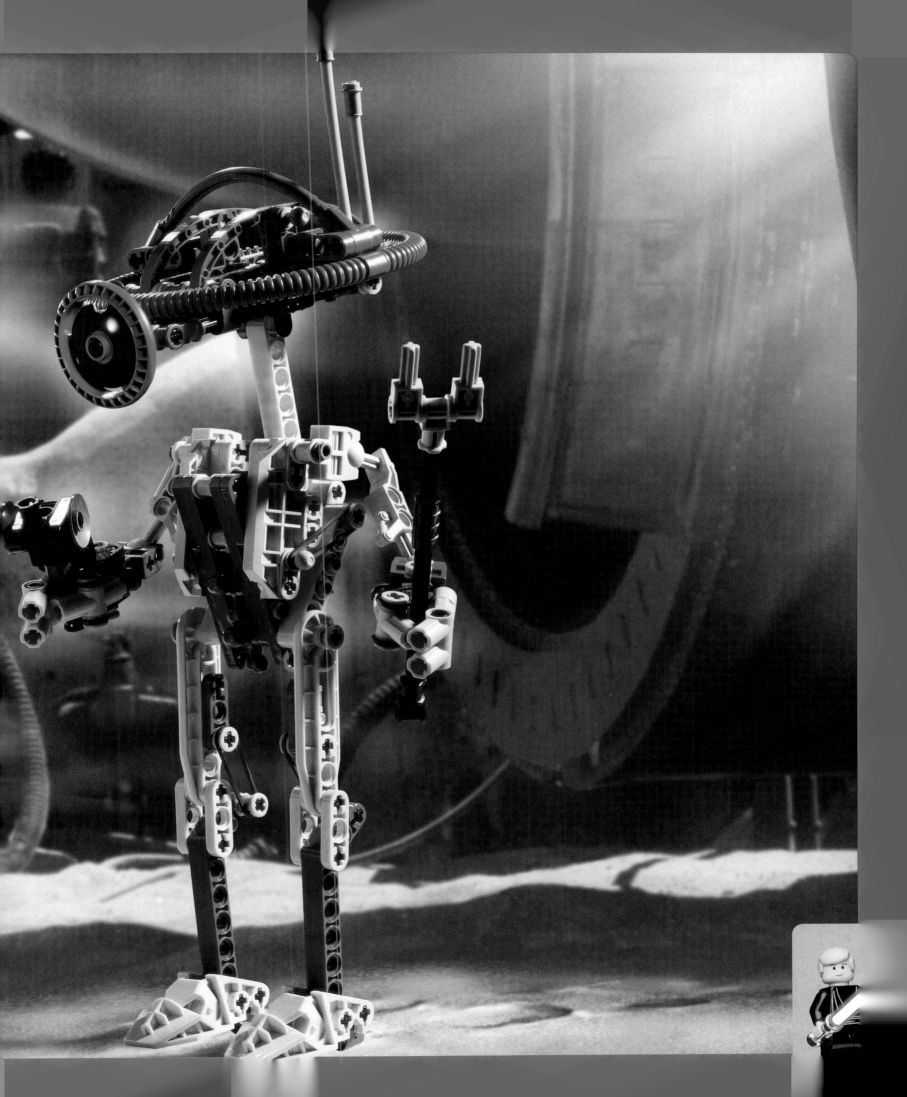

Mini Sets

In 2002, the LEGO Group created the first Mini Sets. They are smaller than the normal sets, with fewer pieces. Though less detailed, Mini Sets are incredibly accurate. The LEGO Group has issued sets to tie in with all six movies and The Clone Wars animation.

3219 TIE FIGHTER (2002)

Printed flap is a unique element

Grey lightsabre blades as guns

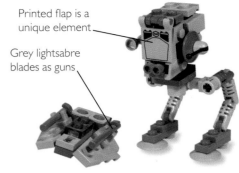

4486 AT-ST & SNOWSPEEDER (2002)

Wings adjust for flight and landing

Printed element

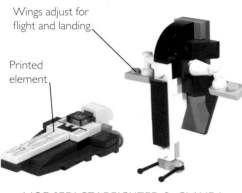

4487 JEDI STARFIGHTER & *SLAVE I* **(2002)**

Both models made from only 76 pieces

Printed tile

S-foils are adjustable

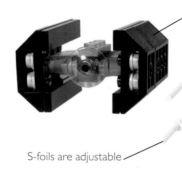

4484 X-WING FIGHTER & TIE ADVANCED (2003)

Energy binders are orange lightsabre blades

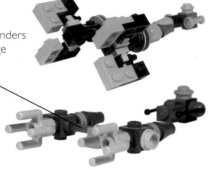

4485 SEBULBA'S PODRACER & ANAKIN'S PODRACER (2003)

Unique printed dish

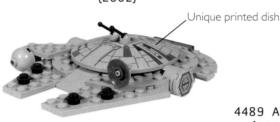

4488 *MILLENNIUM FALCON* **(2003)**

4489 AT-AT (2003)

4490 REPUBLIC GUNSHIP (2003)

Rear hatch opens

Floats on curved pieces

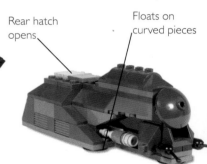

4491 TRADE FEDERATION MTT (2003)

TIE BOMBER (2003)

Y-WING (2003)

Spare pieces issued with four other sets are used to create the TIE Bomber (Sebulba's & Anakin's Podracers; X-wing & TIE Advanced; Jedi Starfighter & *Slave I*; AT-ST & Snowspeeder) and Y-wing (*Millennium Falcon*; AT-AT; Republic Gunship; MTT).

Blaster is a binoculars element

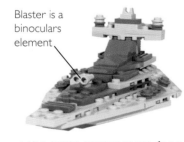

4492 STAR DESTROYER (2004)

Adjustable wing

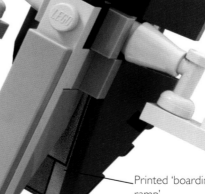

Printed 'boarding ramp'

6964 BOBA FETT'S *SLAVE I* **(2004)**

4494 IMPERIAL SHUTTLE (2003)

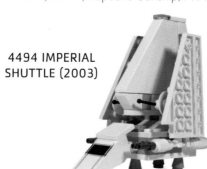

4493 SITH INFILTRATOR (2004)

Cabin screens made of transparent green elements

4495 AT-TE (2004)

6965 TIE INTERCEPTOR (2004)

The TIE Interceptor is an exclusive for certain retailers, including Japanese candy company Kabaya (who sold it with bubblegum!). X-wing (set 6963) and *Slave I* (6964) are also Kabaya exclusives.

Laser cannon (made from lightsabre blade)

6967 ARC FIGHTER (2005)

6966 JEDI STARFIGHTER (2005)

This and Wookiee Attack (set 6968) were only available as instructions on LEGO.com

Comes with clear display stand

8029 REBEL SNOWSPEEDER (2008)

20007 REPUBLIC ATTACK CRUISER (2008)

Hinged wings

8031 V-19 TORRENT (2008)

20006 CLONE TURBO TANK (2008)

Transparent forward viewport

8028 TIE FIGHTER (2008)

BRICK FACTS

● The Mini X-wing appeared first in set 4484 with the TIE Advanced in 2003, and then on its own as a limited-edition exclusive in set 6963.

8033 GENERAL GRIEVOUS'S STARFIGHTER (2009)

20010 REPUBLIC GUNSHIP (2009)

20009 AT-TE (2009)

Drive turbine

30005 IMPERIAL SPEEDER BIKE (2009)

The Imperial speeder bike, STAP and clone walker are all firsts: Mini Sets that are minifigure-sized!

Axe becomes the thrusters!

Drive controls

30004 BATTLE DROID ON STAP (2009)

30006 CLONE WALKER (2009)

LEGO® Technic

LEGO® Technic is an advanced building range that utilises gears and interconnecting rods to create complex models with moving parts. In 2000, the LEGO Group released the first Technic *Star Wars* models, with a pit droid, battle droid and destroyer droid (or droideka). Since then, new Technic sets have appeared for each Prequel Trilogy movie, as well as the Classic Trilogy movies.

▼ Pit Droid

Utilising elastic bands, the pit droid folds up into its compressed form (for storage). A tap on the nose makes the model stand up again.

COMPRESSED FORM

Head plate

Folded limb

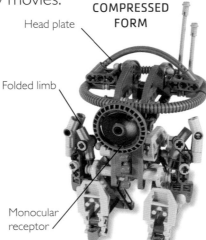

Monocular receptor

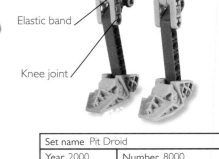

Podracer repair tool

Elastic band

Knee joint

Set name	Pit Droid	
Year 2000	Number 8000	
Pieces 217	Film EP I	

▼ Battle Droid

The battle droid measures over 33 cm (13 inches) tall when standing and can fold up for transportation. When a dial on the back is turned, its arm reaches to the side of its backpack to grab a blaster. The model also comes with spare parts to convert it into a security officer or a commander droid.

Battle droid blaster

Set name	Battle Droid	
Year 2000	Number 8001	
Pieces 328	Film EP I, II & III	

▶ Destroyer Droid

The destroyer droid can fold up into a ball, then, when rolling, it will stop after a few turns and unfold into attack position, with its blasters raised – just like it does in the movie. The model utilises elastic bands in its construction.

Sensor antenna

▶ C-3PO

C-3PO stands 33 cm (13 inches) tall when upright. Just like the scene in *The Empire Strikes Back* when a stormtrooper blasts C-3PO, the model's head and arms blow off (when the 'belly-button' socket is pressed).

Vocoder plate

Set name	Destroyer Droid	
Year 2000	Number 8002	
Pieces 553	Film EP I, II & III	

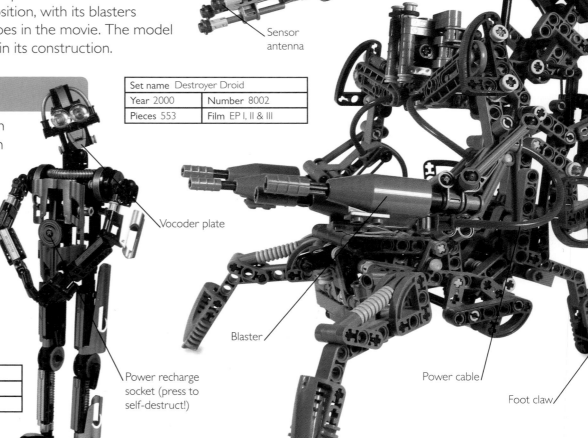

Blaster

Power cable

Foot claw

Set name	C-3PO	
Year 2001	Number 8007	
Pieces 339	Film EP I–VI	

Power recharge socket (press to self-destruct!)

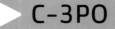

▶ Stormtrooper

The 33-cm (13-inches) tall stormtrooper carries a firing BlasTech E-11 rifle blaster. A wheel in the back allows the arms to move, so the model can aim the blaster – it could even hit C-3PO's socket to blow him up!

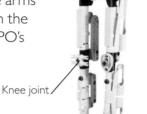

Knee joint

Set name	Stormtrooper	
Year 2001		Number 8008
Pieces 361		Film EP IV, V, & VI

▶ R2-D2

R2-D2 has a rotating dome and, when the front is pressed, his third leg retracts for stability (the other two drive treads also roll). A lever mechanism at the back of the model operates one of R2-D2's utility/repair arms.

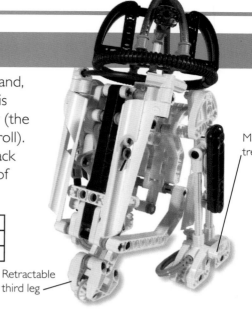

Main drive tread

Set name	R2-D2	
Year 2002		Number 8009
Pieces 242		Film EP I–VI

Retractable third leg

▼ Darth Vader

The Technic model of Darth Vader is armed with his lightsabre, which the figure's hands can grasp and hold. The lightsaber can be raised and lowered using a lever in the back of the model. The cape is made from real cloth.

Set name	Darth Vader	
Year 2002		Number 8010
Pieces 397		Film EP III, IV, V & VI

Sith red eyes

Real fabric cape

▶ Jango Fett

All Jango Fett's limbs and digits (and antenna) are moveable, and a missile can be launched from the jetpack when the model is leaned forward.

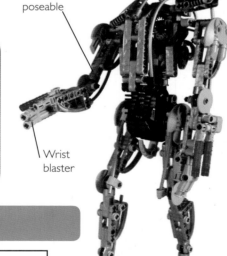

Set name	Jango Fett	
Year 2002		Number 8011
Pieces 429		Film EP II

Blaster

▼ Super Battle Droid

The Super Battle Droid's wrist blasters can be raised and lowered using a lever on the back of the model. The model uses BIONICLE® parts for extra poseability.

Set name	Super Battle Droid	
Year 2002		Number 8012
Pieces 381		Film EP II & III

Eye stalks

All limbs are poseable

Wrist blaster

BRICK FACTS

- In 2008, a Technic model of General Grievous was issued as an Ultimate Collector's Set (set 10186).

- C-3PO and R2-D2 were bundled together as a Toys R Us exclusive (set 65081) in 2002.

▼ Hailfire Droid

This sturdy model of the hailfire droid rolls on its giant hoop wheels. The central blaster gun snaps into place and flick-fires missiles. The model, which is not packaged as a LEGO Technic set, is in proportion to LEGO *Star Wars* minifigures.

Set name	Hailfire Droid	
Year 2003		Number 4481
Pieces 681		Film EP II & III

Missile rack

Hoop drive wheel

Flick-firing blaster gun

83

Ultimate Collector Sets

▼ TIE Interceptor

The TIE Interceptor is captured accurately, with its long dagger-like wings (which can be folded to lie flat) and a hinged cockpit with a detailed interior featuring a pilot seat, controls, a HUD (heads-up display or transparent data screen) and several monitor screens. The model sits on an adjustable stand, which allows it to be displayed in a variety of positions.

The LEGO Group issues a small number of highly detailed *Star Wars* models called Ultimate Collector Sets (or UCS). Intended for older builders and primarily for display, each set includes a collector's card and, in many cases, a display stand. Most are not scaled for minifigures, though some, such as *Millennium Falcon*, are minifigure-scaled.

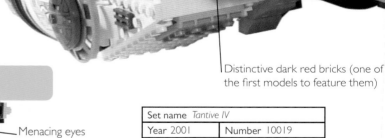

11 engines at the rear

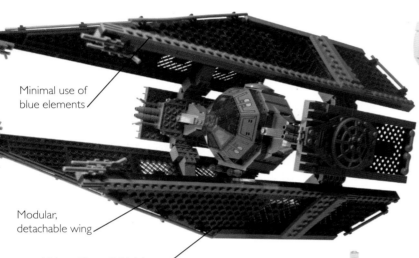

Minimal use of blue elements

Modular, detachable wing

Wings 45 cm (18 in) long

Set name	TIE Interceptor	
Year 2000	Number 7181	
Pieces 703	Film EP VI	

Distinctive dark red bricks (one of the first models to feature them)

Set name	*Tantive IV*	
Year 2001	Number 10019	
Pieces 1,748	Film EP IV	

▷ Darth Maul

The 45-cm (18-inch) tall bust of Sith apprentice Darth Maul has to be constructed from the bottom up and utilises building techniques employed on expert models at LEGOLAND® Parks. This remarkably detailed model weighs almost 4 kg (9 lb).

Menacing eyes

△ Tantive IV

Princess Leia Organa's consular starship, *Tantive IV* (otherwise known as the Blockade Runner), is one of the largest LEGO Ultimate Collector sets, at over 60 cm (2 feet) long and almost 30 cm (1 foot) wide. The highly detailed model is made up of separate sections – front, mid and rear engine block – built individually and then pegged together. The top and lower turbo lasers rotate and the ship is supported on 'landing gear' stands.

Bust can be supported on a special stand

Set name	Darth Maul	
Year 2001	Number 10018	
Pieces 1,868	Film EP I	

Yoda

This sculptural bust of Jedi Grand Master Yoda is an impressive 35.5 cm (14 inches) tall. Like the Darth Maul bust, Yoda is built in layers from the bottom upward: The instructions show a bird's eye view from above rather than a three-dimensional view. When complete, the head can be rotated to different positions.

Flute necklace

Set name	Jedi Master Yoda	
Year 2002	Number 7194	
Pieces 1,075	Film EP I, II, III, V & VI	

BRICK FACTS

- 2000 also saw the release of an UCS X-wing (set 7191), with 1,304 pieces, a gearbox to operate the s-foils, moving controls in the cockpit and an R2-D2 minifigure. The model is nearly 60 cm (2 feet) long, with a wingspan of 45.5 cm (18 inches).

Stickers add details

Naboo Starfighter

Set name	Naboo Starfighter	
Year 2002	Number 10026	
Pieces 187	Film EP I	

R2-D2 (dome only)

Sticker elements

Chrome elements

Sleek finial

Cockpit module slightly larger than movie ship

The Naboo starfighter has fewer bricks than other UCSs, but among them are unique chrome and curved elements, which give the finished model a sleek look. The 29-cm (11.5-inch) long model features twin laser cannons, a proton torpedo launch tube, and R2-D2, as well as a display stand and plaque.

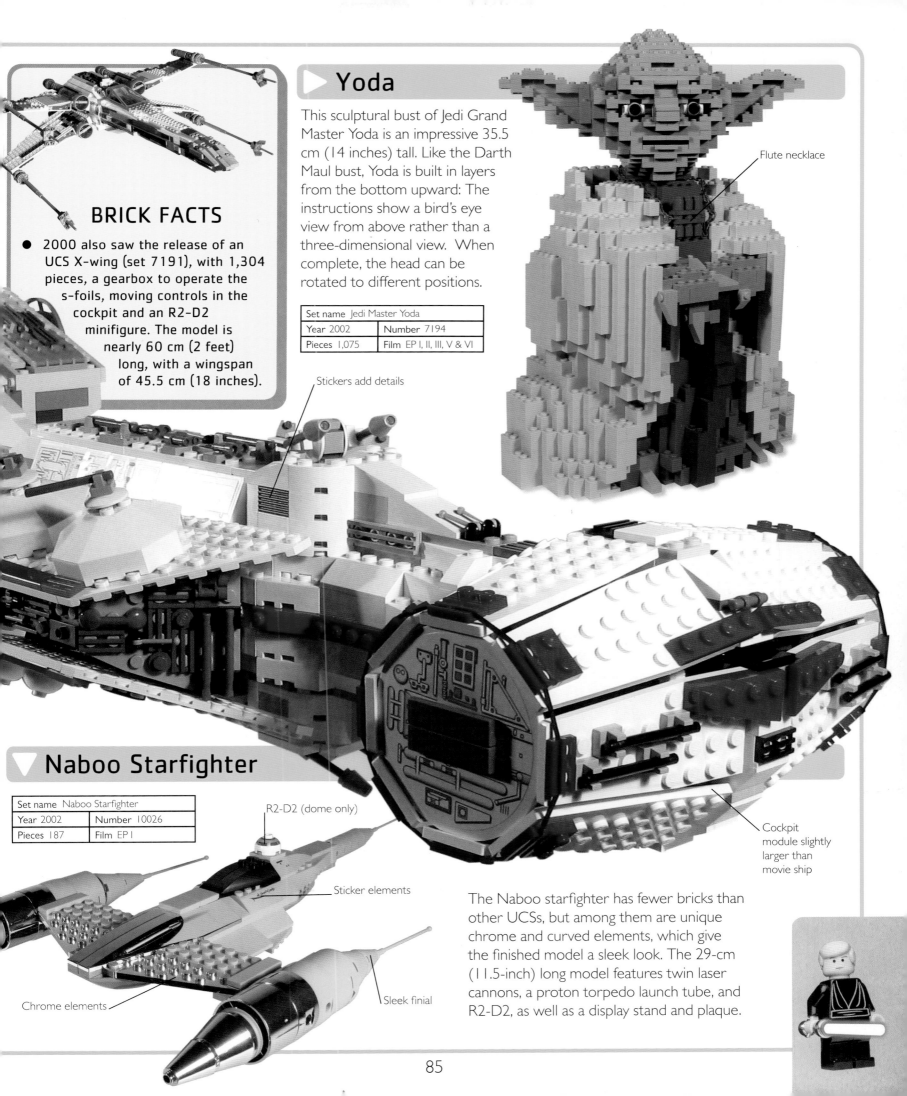

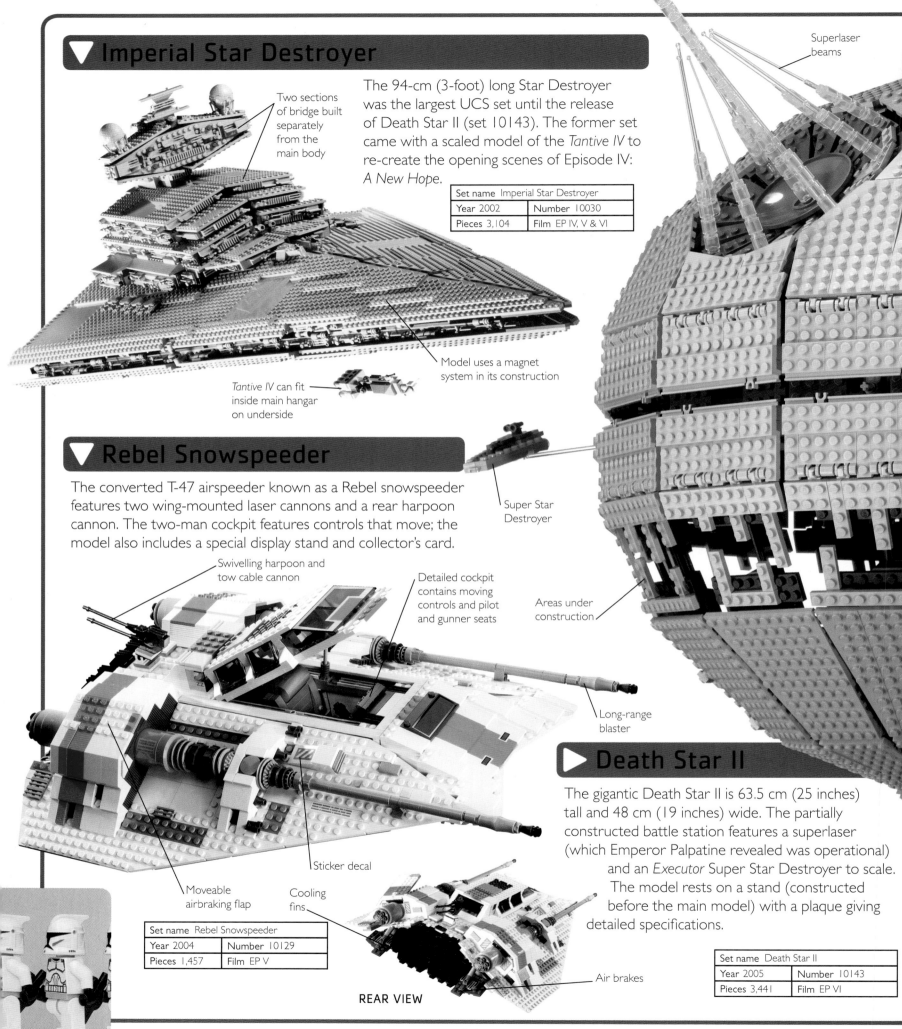

Imperial Star Destroyer

The 94-cm (3-foot) long Star Destroyer was the largest UCS set until the release of Death Star II (set 10143). The former set came with a scaled model of the *Tantive IV* to re-create the opening scenes of Episode IV: *A New Hope.*

Two sections of bridge built separately from the main body

Set name	Imperial Star Destroyer	
Year	2002	Number 10030
Pieces	3,104	Film EP IV, V & VI

Model uses a magnet system in its construction

Tantive IV can fit inside main hangar on underside

Superlaser beams

Super Star Destroyer

Rebel Snowspeeder

The converted T-47 airspeeder known as a Rebel snowspeeder features two wing-mounted laser cannons and a rear harpoon cannon. The two-man cockpit features controls that move; the model also includes a special display stand and collector's card.

Swivelling harpoon and tow cable cannon

Detailed cockpit contains moving controls and pilot and gunner seats

Areas under construction

Long-range blaster

Sticker decal

Moveable airbraking flap

Cooling fins

Set name	Rebel Snowspeeder	
Year	2004	Number 10129
Pieces	1,457	Film EP V

REAR VIEW

Air brakes

Death Star II

The gigantic Death Star II is 63.5 cm (25 inches) tall and 48 cm (19 inches) wide. The partially constructed battle station features a superlaser (which Emperor Palpatine revealed was operational) and an *Executor* Super Star Destroyer to scale. The model rests on a stand (constructed before the main model) with a plaque giving detailed specifications.

Set name	Death Star II	
Year	2005	Number 10143
Pieces	3,441	Film EP VI

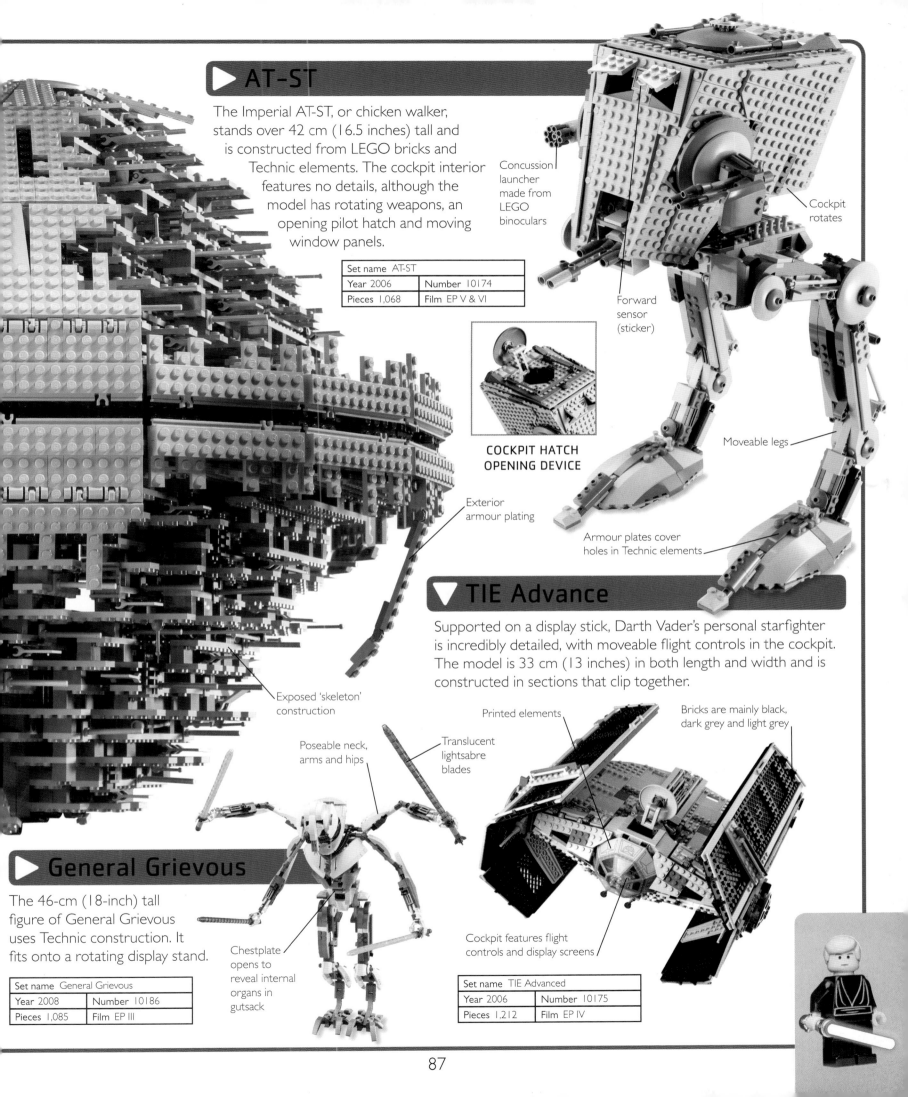

▶ AT-ST

The Imperial AT-ST, or chicken walker, stands over 42 cm (16.5 inches) tall and is constructed from LEGO bricks and Technic elements. The cockpit interior features no details, although the model has rotating weapons, an opening pilot hatch and moving window panels.

Set name	AT-ST	
Year 2006		Number 10174
Pieces 1,068		Film EP V & VI

Concussion launcher made from LEGO binoculars

Cockpit rotates

Forward sensor (sticker)

COCKPIT HATCH OPENING DEVICE

Moveable legs

Exterior armour plating

Armour plates cover holes in Technic elements

Exposed 'skeleton' construction

▼ TIE Advance

Supported on a display stick, Darth Vader's personal starfighter is incredibly detailed, with moveable flight controls in the cockpit. The model is 33 cm (13 inches) in both length and width and is constructed in sections that clip together.

Printed elements

Bricks are mainly black, dark grey and light grey

Poseable neck, arms and hips

Translucent lightsabre blades

▶ General Grievous

The 46-cm (18-inch) tall figure of General Grievous uses Technic construction. It fits onto a rotating display stand.

Chestplate opens to reveal internal organs in gutsack

Cockpit features flight controls and display screens

Set name	General Grievous	
Year 2008		Number 10186
Pieces 1,085		Film EP III

Set name	TIE Advanced	
Year 2006		Number 10175
Pieces 1,212		Film EP IV

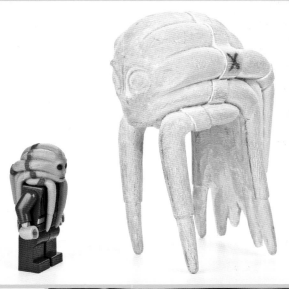

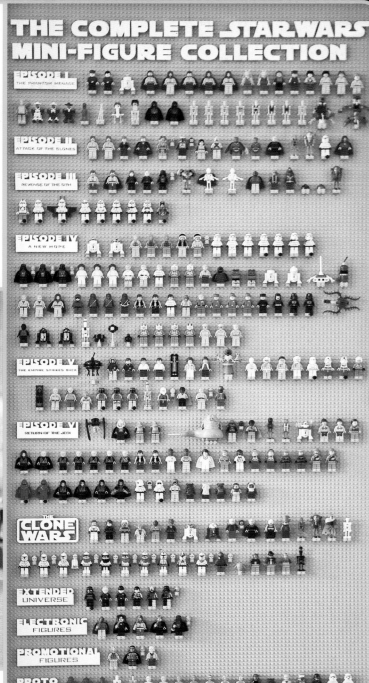

THE COMPLETE STAR WARS MINI-FIGURE COLLECTION

EPISODE I
THE PHANTOM MENACE

EPISODE II
ATTACK OF THE CLONES

EPISODE III
REVENGE OF THE SITH

EPISODE IV
A NEW HOPE

EPISODE V
THE EMPIRE STRIKES BACK

EPISODE VI
RETURN OF THE JEDI

THE CLONE WARS

EXTENDED
UNIVERSE

ELECTRONIC
FIGURES

PROMOTIONAL
FIGURES

PROTO
TYPES

Designing LEGO® *Star Wars*

Jens Kronvold Frederiksen is Design Manager of the LEGO® *Star Wars*™ team in Billund, Denmark. He has worked at the LEGO Group for 11 years, 10 of them in the LEGO *Star Wars* team. He personally created the stunning Ultimate Collector *Millennium Falcon*, as well as many other models. DK interviewed Jens to find out the secrets of how LEGO *Star Wars* is designed.

How big is the Star Wars *team?*

The *Star Wars* team consists of between four and seven designers. We also have project leaders, a marketing leader, engineers developing new elements and building-instruction developers; we all sit in one big group.

The LEGO *Star Wars* design team outside their offices in Billund, Denmark.

Could you explain a little bit about your creative process?

First, we come up with suggestions for models for the various price points. These are presented to the LEGO Group and to the various markets. Lucas Licensing (LFL) also approves the assortment; there might be a vehicle that they recommend because it's in the new *Star Wars: The Clone Wars* TV series.

Then do you start sketching or drawing, or do you build with LEGO bricks?

That is very much up to the designer, because they all work differently. Some designers work best by doing sketches on paper or computer, and some just start building. Normally, I make a brief for the designer. For example, this model should have at least four minifigures – sometimes I know exactly which minifigures and sometimes it's open. I might have some

LEGO *Star Wars* designers at work on the building process.

ideas about the model's functions, but also the designers come up with special features or functions. We then have the 'sketch model' calculated to see if it fits the specific price point. For a very rough idea, we sometimes put the model on a scale and weigh it, as this is actually a pretty good indicator.

Do you have a lot of LEGO bricks, or elements, in your studio?

Yes, we have element drawers behind where we sit, containing all of the elements that are in stock at that time.

How do you decide when to create an entirely new element for a set?

That is something I would put on the design brief. As you also know, many of our new elements are minifigures, so that's very easy to decide beforehand. But sometimes we also know from the beginning whether to construct a specific model with something new. Or a designer will talk to me and say, "I cannot make this model without this new wingtip" or whatever.

Do you often need to amend, change or simplify a sketch model?

It depends. Sometimes if a sketch model is very, very good, it would be a pity to remove some cool functions. We discuss whether we should move the model to a higher price point. But in many cases, the designer simplifies the model or scales it down. Sometimes we even make the models too inexpensively, so we then add extra functions or figures and so on. But now, with the experience that we have got, it's normally pretty close.

How long does it take to design a sketch model?

That depends on the size of the model. A mini model can take an afternoon, but can also take a week. A big model like the *Tantive IV* can take a couple of months. Sometimes

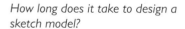

An early model of the Trade Federation Shuttle based on concept reference. It was later changed to match new reference.

we make models that we don't use straight away, but we still keep everything.

What is the next stage in the design process?

We have something called Model Review. This is a process in which very skilled or experienced designers from outside the *Star Wars* team work with our designer, engineers, building-instruction developers and everyone involved in the model. Together, they ensure that the model can be shown in the building instructions in an understandable way. We also test the technical quality – to ensure the model does not fall apart and that there are no elements that are stretched and then could break.

We also normally heat test the models! Because if you take a LEGO model and display it in your window, in the sun, it will get to pretty high temperatures. Plastic is a funny material as it actually expands in the heat, which means the bricks will be a little bit more loose. Therefore, we take the model and put in an oven at 60 degrees Celsius for about four hours, which is the same stress as if a model were standing for about a year in a window.

The big Ultimate Collectors *Millennium Falcon* was too big for the oven! So we called a local swimming pool that had a sauna and we brought the model in and put it there for some hours, and it worked!

When all the internal quality issues are okay, I send lots of pictures of the model with a long description to LFL. Sometimes we make small movie clips to show functions. Occasionally, we also send them physical models – it depends on how complex the model is. But normally it's just pictures.

And then LFL evaluates it from a Star Wars *point of view?*

They evaluate it by comparing it to their official reference, which we also use. They are very particular about the outside but are normally quite open about the inside. Like us, LFL is very aware that the models are actually toys and do have to be fun, so sometimes we will put something in the interior that is not actually in the movies, just because it is fun.

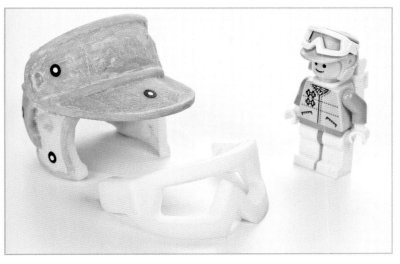

A 3:1 scale prototype of the 2009 Hoth Rebel soldier's helmet. It is hand-sculpted in modelling clay, which is then baked in an oven to harden it. The prototype is digitally scanned and the resulting image used to make the actual mould for the production of the final plastic elements.

Can you give an example?

The Gungan Sub, for example. That model could actually be taken apart and used as three separate vehicles, which it obviously couldn't do in the movie. Also, in the new Mon Cal Cruiser, Admiral Ackbar has a coffee mug beside him on the railing!

Which models were most challenging to design?

Many different things can be challenging – it could be the building instructions or it could be the stability of the model. From the models I have designed myself, such as the UCS *Millennium Falcon*, getting the stability right was the hardest thing. The exterior of this particular model was pretty close to the first sketch model. The big problem was the inside skeleton, which had to be reconstructed a couple of times to make it strong enough.

An unreleased sketch model of the Rebel Base on Yavin 4. Designers in the LEGO *Star Wars* team make many product suggestions and keep all their sketch models, even when, as is the case with this one, there are no plans to issue them as sets.

Did this particular model take a lot longer than normal to design?

It is hard to say because I actually started it outside of work, just for fun. I was aware that a real *Millennium Falcon* should fit four minifigures in the cockpit. None of the previous play model versions had a big enough cockpit. When I was halfway through the process, the LEGO shop came by and saw it and decided it would be interesting to sell it at a higher price point. Then I was given the most amazing brief: They let me make the model the way I wanted it first and they priced it afterward!

Are you all Star Wars *fans?*

Well, not everyone, but the designers are normally big fans. If they weren't, they would not be able to come up with and create the best products for the brand. They know all these small details, so it is definitely an interest.

Do you regularly test models by asking children to play with them?

Yes. We ask in a group of children from the correct age group and just let them play with the sketch models. We observe the kids playing without interfering. It's quite easy to spot a model that no one is playing with. We can also see if a model breaks apart too easily or is too hard to make. You always have to have the kids in mind. With the Ultimate Collectors Series, it's about having something nice to display, but with the minifigure-based models, they just have to be good toys.

Finally, would you tell me something about the exclusive Luke Skywalker minifigure that comes with this book?

One of our graphic designers, Chris Bonven Johansen, designed the minifigure after LFL suggested adding an exclusive one to the book. We had a brainstorming session in the team and proposed Luke because this book is a celebration, and the minifigure comes from the celebration scene in *Star Wars*: Episode IV *A New Hope*, so it couldn't fit better. I am also sure that this minifigure will never appear with any other product, so it's a great choice!

One of the most 'precious' element drawers – containing the newest minifigure parts!

Merchandising

LEGO® *Star Wars*™ is not just about bricks and pieces – fans can also dress the part and accessorise themselves (and their fridges) to match. Much of the LEGO *Star Wars* merchandise incorporates construction or play elements, such as watches you can build and customisable pens. Adult collectors can make grown-up-sized watches and special maquette minifigures – strictly for display, not play!

Poseable, removeable head held on with magnets

BOBA FETT (2007)

▶ Maquettes

California-based model-making company Gentle Giant Studios created a series of 15.25-cm (6-inch) limited-edition maquettes based on LEGO *Star Wars* videogame characters. As a surprise extra, some Vader maquettes came with a spare grey Anakin Skywalker head and a few stormtroopers also had a Han Solo head!

Maquettes made of polyresin

BLACKHOLE TROOPER (2007)

STORMTROOPER (2007)

▽ Key Chains

If you want to keep safe the keys to your starfighter, then these key chains are just what you need! Characters available include Darth Vader, Yoda and Count Dooku.

ages/edades **6+** 851683 0-3

Ages/edades **6+**

Asajj Ventress™

0-3

ASAJJ VENTRESS (2008)

Carabiner-style clip

R2-D2 (2005)

©2005 LFL and the LEGO Group.

LEGO logo tile

ROYAL GUARD (2005)

DARTH VADER (2007)

▽ Bag Charms

JEDI STARFIGHTER™
Exclusive Bag Charm
Ages/
edades
6+

Bigger than key chains, bag charms feature minivehicles rather than minifigures. Choose from a Jedi starfighter, a Y-wing starfighter, Luke Skywalker's landspeeder, Darth Vader's TIE fighter, *Slave I* or the *Millennium Falcon*.

Decorative tin

▽ Watches

LEGO *Star Wars* watches are available in child and adult sizes. Like a LEGO model, they must be built: Strap links are snapped together in any combination then joined to the face and clasp.

Strap links

LEGO minifigure on face

Sturdy clasp

Strap links to create different patterns and sizes

STORMTROOPER
ADULT WATCH (2009)

Luke Skywalker minifigure

50m/165ft

LUKE SKYWALKER
WATCH (2007)

▽ Video Games

LEGO *Star Wars: The Video Game* allows gamers to play through the action of Episodes I–III as any of 56 minifigures, from Obi-Wan Kenobi to a GNK Droid! It was followed in 2006 by LEGO *Star Wars* II: The Original Trilogy.

▽ Magnets

You'll never lose the secret Death Star plans if you stick them to the fridge door with one of these extra cool minifigure magnets.

Minifigures come with accessories

CHEWBACCA
MAGNET (2009)

▽ Pens

The original packaging for the Anakin Skywalker pen had an accidental spelling mistake: 'Skywlaker'. A corrected pen was released, but it is the rarer of the two versions.

Arms can move

Pens can be customised

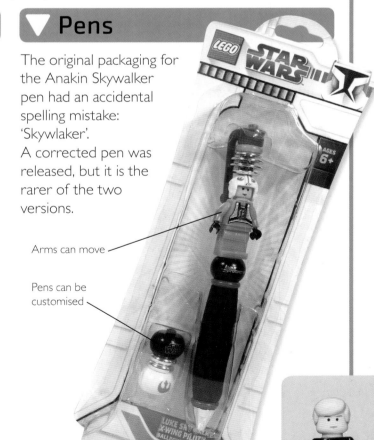

X-WING LUKE
PEN (2009)

Community

The LEGO® fan community spans generations, reaches across continents and bridges languages. The simple brick has been transformed into the most creative and versatile construction element in the world, and, as each day goes by, even more ingenious uses are devised.

▼ Fan Events

All around the world LEGO *Star Wars* fans get together in small venues or giant conventions centres to share their latest creations and encourage fellow builders. The LEGO Group often attends these events to showcase new sets and interact with its many enthusiastic fans.

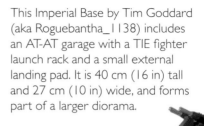

Regular set inside special slipcase

In 2005, at the New York Toy Fair, attendees of the LEGO Group's V.I.P. gala event received a special edition of the Darth Vader transformation set. At the 2009 New York Toy Fair, lucky guests received a chrome Darth Vader minifigure in an exclusive box.

Rotating turbolaser turrets

Steel support frame

GIANT REPUBLIC STAR DESTROYER

In 2005, the LEGO Group commissioned employee Erik Varszegi to build a massive 2.4-meter (8-foot) *Venator*-class Star Destroyer for the *Star Wars Celebration III* convention. The model contains 35,000 bricks, weighs close to 68 kg (150 lbs) and takes four people to lift it.

▼ Fan Creations

The beauty of LEGO bricks is that you can make just about anything with them, and groups of expert builders, or AFOLs (Adult Fans of LEGO), do just that. Their custom designs even have their own specialist term: MOCs (My Own Creations)!

IMPERIAL BASE

This Imperial Base by Tim Goddard (aka Roguebantha_1138) includes an AT-AT garage with a TIE fighter launch rack and a small external landing pad. It is 40 cm (16 in) tall and 27 cm (10 in) wide, and forms part of a larger diorama.

Right-hand turret operates launch rack

Launch rack slides forward for rapid TIE deployment

Doors slide open along sunken groove tracks

AT-AT garage

Official five-minute brickfilm from 2005

LEGO® *STAR WARS*™ ONLINE

With over 2.5 million registered users, LEGO.com is a lot more than just an online store. The LEGO Group uploads brickfilms (short animated movies) and movie-comics, while fans can post their own brickfilms and creations.

Many movie-accurate details (these Stormtroopers are searching for missing droids)

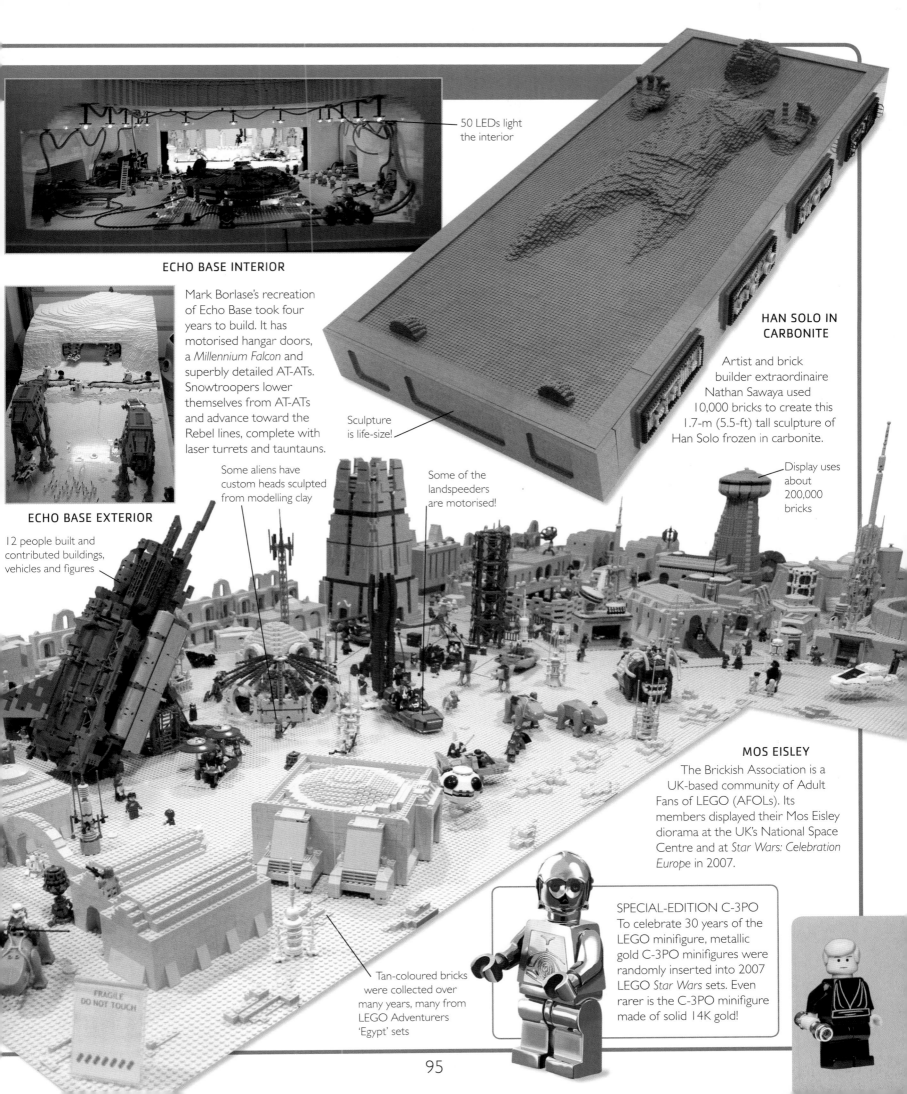

ECHO BASE INTERIOR

50 LEDs light the interior

Mark Borlase's recreation of Echo Base took four years to build. It has motorised hangar doors, a *Millennium Falcon* and superbly detailed AT-ATs. Snowtroopers lower themselves from AT-ATs and advance toward the Rebel lines, complete with laser turrets and tauntauns.

HAN SOLO IN CARBONITE

Artist and brick builder extraordinaire Nathan Sawaya used 10,000 bricks to create this 1.7-m (5.5-ft) tall sculpture of Han Solo frozen in carbonite.

Sculpture is life-size!

ECHO BASE EXTERIOR

12 people built and contributed buildings, vehicles and figures

Some aliens have custom heads sculpted from modelling clay

Some of the landspeeders are motorised!

Display uses about 200,000 bricks

MOS EISLEY

The Brickish Association is a UK-based community of Adult Fans of LEGO (AFOLs). Its members displayed their Mos Eisley diorama at the UK's National Space Centre and at *Star Wars: Celebration Europe* in 2007.

Tan-coloured bricks were collected over many years, many from LEGO Adventurers 'Egypt' sets

SPECIAL-EDITION C-3PO
To celebrate 30 years of the LEGO minifigure, metallic gold C-3PO minifigures were randomly inserted into 2007 LEGO *Star Wars* sets. Even rarer is the C-3PO minifigure made of solid 14K gold!

FRAGILE DO NOT TOUCH

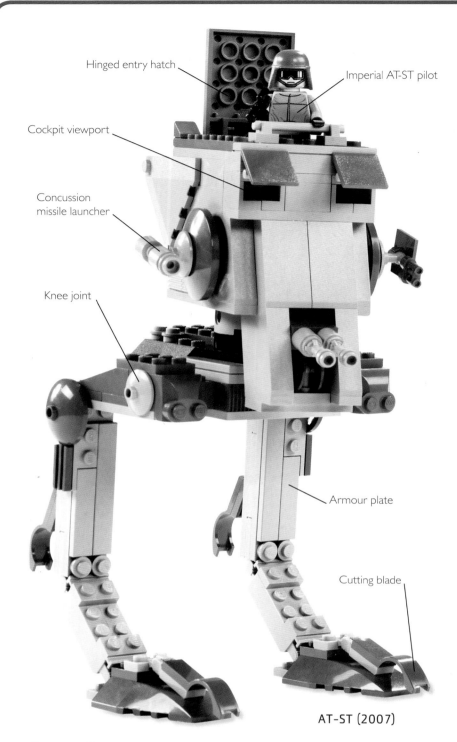

Hinged entry hatch

Imperial AT-ST pilot

Cockpit viewport

Concussion
missile launcher

Knee joint

Armour plate

Cutting blade

AT-ST (2007)

LONDON, NEW YORK, MUNICH,
MELBOURNE and DELHI

Project Editor Elizabeth Dowsett
Designer Jon Hall
Managing Editor Catherine Saunders
Art Director Lisa Lanzarini
Category Publisher Alex Allan
Production Controller Nick Seston
Production Editor Clare McLean

Additional design for DK by Dan Bunyan

First published in the Great Britain in 2009
by Dorling Kindersley Limited,
80 Strand, London WC2R 0RL

6 8 10 9 7 5
175451—07/09

Discover more at
www.dk.com
www.lego.com
www.starwars.com

Acknowledgements

The author would like to thank the following
people: Stephanie Lawrence at the LEGO Group and
Carol Roeder and Jonathan Rinzler at Lucas Licensing,
for allowing me to write this book, and their
colleagues, art director Troy Alders and Keeper of
the Holocron, Leland Chee; Alex Allan at DK, for
allowing me the time to write this book (and for the
minifigures!); Randi Sørensen at the LEGO Group,
who was an ever-helpful champion and approver of
the book; Keith Malone at the LEGO Group for the
initial treatment; Jon Hall – designer, LEGO fan, and
animator (he made the flip-animation work!);

Elizabeth Dowsett, for being a tireless project
editor and calm voice of reason; Jeremy Beckett,
for ensuring accuracy and supplying photos of his
extensive collection (Jeremy, I wish I could get you
a 2009 Toy Fair Vader!); Jens Kronvold Frederiksen for
talking to me about his enviable job, and of course,
for creating – with his team – all the incredible LEGO
models that fill these pages; Hannah Collins, for
transcribing the interview; to my wife, Katie, for gently
humouring me in my enthusiasm for this project; finally,
this book is dedicated to Linus and Edie Beecroft and
Max Parker, LEGO fans who are actually still kids.

PICTURE CREDITS
Images supplied by the LEGO Group. Additional
photography by Jeremy Beckett and Sarah Ashun.
Page 94: right © Tim Goddard; Page 95: top left and
middle left © Mark Borlase/Brickplumber; top right,
Han Solo in Carbonite sculpture by artist, Nathan
Sawaya. Photo courtesy of brickartist.com; middle
and bottom right © Ian Greig, 2007

Thanks also to Erik Varszegi, who built the giant
Republic Star Destroyer (page 94).